Coping Behaviors
and Nursing

LaRetta M. Garland, R.N., Ed.D.

Carol T. Bush, R.N., Ph.D.

Nell Hodgson Woodruff School of Nursing
Emory University
Atlanta, Georgia

WY
87
.G233c
1982

Reston Publishing Company, Inc.
Reston, Virginia
A Prentice-Hall Company

The content presented in this book reflects the views of the authors and is not necessarily endorsed by the Nell Hodgson Woodruff School of Nursing of Emory University.

Figures 2-1 to 2-8 are from T. Randall Lankford, *Integrated Science for Health Students*, second edition. ©1979 by Reston Publishing Company, Inc. Illustrations by Richard T. Kirksey.

Library of Congress Cataloging in Publication Data
Garland, LaRetta M.
    Coping behaviors and nursing.

    Bibliography: p.
    Includes index.
    1. Nursing—Psychological aspects.   2. Adjustment
(Psychology)   I. Bush, Carol T.   II. Title.
[DNLM: 1. Adaptation, Psychological—Nursing
texts.   2. Psychology—Nursing texts.   3. Stress,
Psychological—Nursing texts.   WY 87 G233c]
RT86.G37   155.9'16'024613   81-17770
ISBN 0-87909-088-X   AACR2
        0-87909-089-8 (pbk)

© 1982 by
Reston Publishing Company, Inc.
Reston, Virginia 22090

10   9   8   7   6   5   4   3   2   1

PRINTED IN THE UNITED STATES OF AMERICA

Contents

Preface

This book is designed to provide nurses with a conceptual approach for identifying and responding to frequently encountered coping behaviors. The authors distinguish between adaptive and maladaptive coping mechanisms; provide definitions and descriptions of closely related terms and give examples of each; and discuss psychological and physiological stressors and responses. Implications for education, consultation, and research are included.

The content is designed to enable students in schools of nursing and nurses practicing in a variety of situations to be aware of coping behaviors and plan appropriate interventions as indicated. Coping behaviors should be assessed according to their potential adaptability in assisting clients to meet their goals. Maladaptive coping behaviors should be modified or extinguished, and adaptive ones should be strengthened when they appear to facilitate the accomplishment of individuals' and society's goals.

Using this book as a supplementary text, undergraduate students can be helped to understand clients' physiological and psychological responses in relation to current situations and past behaviors. Graduate students can use the text as a reference

for definitions of key concepts and a basis for designing research. Nurses in practice will find a new way of viewing clients
and themselves that should be enlightening and motivating.

The authors express their appreciation to their families,
teachers, students, and clients who have taught them to cope.
Also, the authors extend gratitude to the readers of the man-
uscript, including Drs. Ellen Fuller and Leah Gorman and Ms.
Susan Seamons.

LaRetta M. Garland

Carol T. Bush

Foreword

In an era of rapid cultural transition, increasing societal diversity, complex technology, and systems breakdown, people are stressed nearly beyond endurance. It is both fitting and timely that two highly qualified nurse-educators have collaborated in writing a book on coping behaviors for the health professional.

With a refreshing originality, Dr. LaRetta M. Garland, a counselor and adult health nurse, and Dr. Carol Bush, a psychiatric-mental health nurse, have merged their expertise on the psyche and the soma in a pragmatic presentation of stress and coping.

This publication is unique in its reality-oriented approach to a subject that is too often clouded by esoteric language and in its practical applicability, which is reinforced by a variety of case histories.

The authors have provided a detailed differentiation between adaptive and maladaptive coping patterns. Their comprehensive discussion of models of intervention is conceptually sound and provides clear direction for professional practice.

The book is a needed resource for nurses and other health professionals.

M. Leah Gorman, Ed.D., R.N.

Chapter 1

Definitions of Coping and Related Concepts

REASONS FOR STUDYING COPING

There are three primary reasons why the concept of coping should be a serious consideration of health care professionals. First, it is critical for professionals who work with clients to identify the coping behaviors exhibited by their clients and assess whether those behaviors are potentially adaptive or maladaptive. In other words, caregivers should make some judgment as to whether the exhibited (or implied) behaviors will have potential for healthy or unhealthy consequences. Based on the assessment, the coping behaviors should be either reinforced or extinguished, or other behaviors should be substituted.

The second reason for health professionals to be familiar with coping processes is that the caregivers themselves are frequently in stressful situations. They must make decisions that will affect the lives of their clients and clients' families indefinitely. Therefore, it behooves those who are responsible for the care of others to try to develop insight into their own coping behaviors and the consequences of those behaviors.

A nurse, for example, happened to be near the scene of an automobile accident in which the driver of one of the vehicles was trapped in the car. The nurse performed superbly in assessing the seriousness of the situation, calling an ambulance, directing bystanders to gather equipment, instructing others in the process of freeing the victim, and attempting to administer emergency care. In spite of all of the efforts of the nurse, the victim was pronounced dead on arrival at the emergency room at a nearby hospital. Coping in this situation was difficult for the nurse. She had spent her best efforts in the fast-moving endeavor, to no avail. Afterwards she spent time in an extensive mental review of the details of the whole process, trying to determine what she could have performed differently. Such a review was appropriate; the nurse had a support system wherein someone was willing to listen to her and realistically comment that she had indeed done all that could have been done. If, for a variety of reasons, the nurse had let the incident interfere with her subsequent functioning as a nurse or as an individual, the reaction might have been considered exaggerated and maladaptive. Thus, a nurse must learn appropriate means of coping with his or her own abilities, limitations, and personal expectations as well as with those of clients who receive the nurse's services. Moreover, the nurse or other caregiver must deal with the same sets of variables presented by other personnel and families in health care settings.

The third reason for health professionals to learn more about the coping process probably has longer-range and broader implications than the other two, for it relates to the need for systematic investigation into how individuals, families, and groups cope. What determines which coping behaviors an individual will use? What are the consequences of the various coping behaviors? What can be done to facilitate the utilization of healthy coping behaviors? What can be done to eliminate or minimize the utilization of unhealthy coping behaviors? Research along these lines would be exciting, for it could involve an interdisciplinary approach if done as quasi-experimental field research. The results could have far-reaching implications.

NURSING AS A FRAMEWORK FOR EXAMINATION OF COPING

The framework for this examination of coping and its implications for nursing will be the nursing process. The nursing process may be divided into four steps: (a) assessing the patient, significant others, and the environment; (b) planning the best possible strategy to maximize adaptation; (c) implementing the plan; and (d) evaluating the results. While the process is circular in that further plans for intervention are based on the evaluation, the process must always start with the assessment. This first chapter addresses definitions of *coping* and related terms in order to provide a base from which assessments may be made using terminology that has been clarified for this purpose. Likewise, Chapter 2 presents foundational material that is included to help the reader comprehend the biophysical-psychosocial influences on coping behavior. Chapter 3 deals specifically with assessment and includes tools that may be used in assessing a patient's coping behaviors. Planning and implementing are covered in Chapter 4, which includes a number of possible interventions that might be used to enhance the individual's coping effectiveness. Evaluation involves reassessing the patient after some intervention has been instigated. For individual clients, therefore, evaluation involves the same procedures as those used in the initial assessment in order to determine what changes have been effected. In a broader sense, however, evaluation involves systematic research to investigate the effectiveness of various interventions and programs of care. Chapter 5 addresses the issue of research as well as consultation and education.

COPING AND THE NURSE'S ROLE

In this era of emphasis on holistic health care it is fitting that the nurse should lead the way in providing comprehensive health care, for the nurse has been concerned for the "whole patient" even while responding to the demands for increased knowledge and the necessity of specialization. Since coping strategies are a significant factor in a patient's health—including health maintenance, response to illness, and compliance to health-restoring regimens—the importance of strengthening the patient's coping behaviors seems obvious. Equally important is the nurse's role in providing the patient with an environment in which his or her coping behaviors may be utilized and strengthened, or, if lacking, may be learned.

COPING AND RELATED TERMS

Coping is a term that is currently enjoying widespread use. Individuals are wearing T-shirts with the inscription "Don't bother me, I can't cope." Books, pamphlets, lectures, seminars, and discussions are advertised on how to cope with life, death, college, divorce, inflation, illness in the family, or an alcoholic spouse—to name only a few. Because it is so widely used, *coping* must be defined here specifically as it applies to the discussions in this book. In addition, there are many related terms closely associated with coping that must be clarified. For historical perspective and because they are widely recognized coping devices, the defense mechanisms will be discussed. That discussion will be followed by a consideration of the psychological implications of stress (physiological aspects of stress are reviewed in Chapter 2). *Adaptation* will be defined and differentiated from coping, followed by a discussion of the concepts of *threat, appraisal,* and *crisis. Mastery, resiliency,* and *adjustment* are some of the other terms that emerge in the coping literature, and they will be reviewed. Coping will be considered both in relation to these other terms and in its uniqueness.

Coping

Coping is the process by which an individual attempts to alleviate, attentuate, or remove stress or threat; this process may consist of a rather large array of covert and overt behaviors (McGrath, 1970). In other words, coping is what people do when they have a problem (Aguilera & Messick, 1974), the efforts they make to meet threats (Lazarus, 1966). It is important, however, that in attempting to define and clarify coping, we do not lose sight of the complexity of the concept. Coping is an interaction of individuals and environment. The reaction an individual has to an environmental event is as important as the event itself (Lazarus & Launier, 1978). Therefore, not only does a person's coping ability have implications for mental and physical health, but the person's state of health likewise influences coping responses (Antonovsky, 1979; Lazarus & Launier, 1978).

The coping process can occur in *anticipation* of a threat; that is, behavior may be executed because one believes that there is going to be a threat (which, of course, *is* a threat). Planning includes the goal of meeting the demands of the stressful situation when and if it occurs. Firedrills might be an example of anticipatory coping. On the other hand, *preventive coping* seeks to avoid the threatening event. Proper wiring and other fire safety precautions are examples of preventive coping (McGrath, 1970). Anticipatory coping may be more difficult for individuals than is coping with the real event. Lazarus (1966) used the example of the examination period, in which the student has a much looser situation in preparing for an exam than he does at the actual time of taking the exam. Preparation encompasses a wide range of activities such as reviewing class notes, reading the text, working problems, discussing the topics with other students, and many other options. In contrast, during the examination the student has a more limited number of options: He can think, write, or give up and hand the paper in blank.

Anticipatory coping behaviors, if overdone, can lead to difficulties. When repeatedly exposed to threatening situations that require the execution of coping behaviors, an individual begins to anticipate the harmful situation and institute the coping behaviors before the event occurs. If that individual repeats this process to the point of consistently reacting in an emergency fashion, behavior will become stereotyped, and the individual will become unable to react spontaneously to the real environment. The behavior designed to protect will, in fact, deny pleasure and perpetuate anguish (Millon, 1969).

Sexual problems, which often develop in this manner, are an illustration of this process. For example, a man may be unable to achieve an erection on one occasion because of environmental factors, which could include overindulgence in alcohol, extreme fatigue, or job pressures. The memory of such a failure will cause him to *anticipate* that he may not be able to have an erection the next time he has the opportunity to engage in sexual intercourse, and this anticipation will cause such stress that he, in fact, will fail again. It is easy to understand how the successive failures compound the problem by increasing the man's anxiety: He fears (or anticipates) failure, which makes it impossible for him to succeed, and the vicious cycle continues.

Students who have difficulty taking an examination are another example of anticipatory attempts at coping leading to a compounding of the problem rather than a solution. A student who is anxious about taking tests will often anticipate failure, which will increase anxiety so that performing in the test-taking situation is difficult and leads to low test scores and increased anxiety about test-taking. The vicious cycle is thus created.

Factors Involved in Coping Strategies

McGrath (1970) identified four factors involved in the strategies of coping. *Time* is a factor in the coping process, particularly with relation to the interval between the time of onset of the cues that lead to the anticipation of the threatening event and the actual occurrence of the harmful event. Another critical time period is that between the initiation of the coping behaviors and the expected time of results or alleviation of the stress. If an automobile accident is impending, the driver swerves to avert the collision and is instantly reinforced by the relief of the threatening situation. However, for the person trying to lose weight, the results typically take too long to be effective, and the behaviors instituted to relieve the individual of excess bulk are abandoned (McGrath, 1970).

The second factor identified by McGrath (1970)—the *goal* of the coping behavior—is influential in that coping efforts are directed toward preventing or removing the threat, as mentioned previously, or toward removing or attenuating the consequences of the threatening situation. If one is injured, for example, one may have to deal with the results of the injury long after the injury-causing event has passed (McGrath, 1970).

The third factor identified by McGrath (1970) is that of the *effectiveness* of the coping behaviors used. This factor becomes very important to people who attempt to help others, for the effectiveness of what the patient or client is doing for himself or herself must be assessed before a decision can be made as to whether the behavior should be reinforced or extinguished. McGrath noted how complicated it is to make such an assessment. The effectiveness is determined by whether or not the behavior accomplishes its goal of removing the threat or its consequences. However, the cost to the individual must also be evaluated, and this determination is not without value judgments. Chapter 3 provides more discussion of the differentiation between effective and ineffective coping behaviors.

The *number of coping strategies used* at a given time or in response to a given threat, as well as in various situations, is the fourth coping factor. Flexibility has been considered to be the ideal (McGrath, 1970; Millon, 1969). Indeed, Lazarus and Launier (1978), Pearlin and Schooler (1978), and others (Felton, Brown, Lehmann, & Liberatos, 1980) indicated that stability is a limited part of coping because changes are inevitable. It is desirable to keep trying alternatives, thus increasing variability of responses. On the other hand, there is evidence that individuals who are consistent in the coping behaviors they employ are freer according to such indicators of stress as skin conductances and decision times (Steiner, 1970). Questions are increasingly being raised about the desirability of being flexible versus having some dependable coping behaviors to rely on. The clinical and research implications for health-care professionals are crucial: Can an individual be taught new coping behaviors? Are there coping behaviors that are specific for some individuals in some situations but contraindicated for others or in different situations? Do individuals have limits as to the number of coping behaviors they can use effectively? The answers to these and related questions will increase the professional's effectiveness in the improvement of services rendered to clients.

The characteristics of coping are generally listed in positive terms, thus implying effective coping behaviors. Since there is usually some choice of behaviors to use in coping, coping is considered to be flexible in addition to being goal-oriented. Although it is somewhat future-oriented, coping also includes the responses of the individual to the needs of the present and the reality of the current environment. Individuals are generally conscious of what they are doing, and they vary their responses appropriately according to situational changes. In contrast to expecting difficulties to disappear magically, coping individuals face reality and work within the difficulties if they cannot eliminate them. Coping individuals allow themselves pleasurable gratification of drives in open and appropriate manners (Haan, 1963; Lazarus, 1966).

Examples of Coping Behaviors

The examples of coping behaviors are almost infinite and include such behaviors as thinking things out, talking things out, confronting those with whom one disagrees, avoiding situations that have potential for conflict, structuring one's activities, exercising to "work out tensions," and seeking professional help for solving one's problems (Aguilera & Messick, 1974). Gazda (1971) identified coping behaviors for the developmental stages, including the young child's coping with drives toward independence by learning rudimentary safety rules; the early adolescent's coping with social groups by overconforming to peer rules; or the older person's coping with decreasing physical strength by limiting activities. This list of developmental coping behaviors is expanded in Chapter 3.

The question arises as to what determines which coping behaviors an individual will choose to employ in a given threatening situation. The process of deciding on which coping options and resources to use has been labeled *secondary appraisal* (Lazarus, 1966; Lazarus & Launier, 1978).* Three classes of factors are involved in secondary appraisal: degree of threat, factors in the stimulus configuration, and the individual's appraisal of how harmful the event might be as well as how imminent the occurrence of the event is. Factors in the stimulus configuration include how obvious the source of the threat is or whether the problem has been appropriately defined, as well as the coping options available and the relevant environmental constraints. The decision the individual makes has to do with degree of motivation, including what price the individual is willing to pay for relief, degree of ego strength, and resources for dealing with the environment as one assesses it. Millon

---

*See Threat and Appraisal, pages 25–26.

(1969) also cited three primary determinants of choice of coping strategy that are not significantly different from those proposed by Lazarus, although the groupings might be different. Millon's determinants are the individual's inborn capacities and dispositions, history of stimulus reinforcements, and the realistic alternatives currently available.

Categories of Coping Resources

Coping resources may be either internal or external (Wheaton, 1980). Internal coping resources are learned individual responses due to a person's ability or effort or a combination of both. External coping resources include an individual's social support network (p.102). More specifically, there are at least five categories of coping resources:

1. *Health/energy/morale*, imply that a sickly, weak, despondent person would have more difficulty coping than one who is healthy, strong, and optimistic.
2. *Problem solving skills* at both concrete and abstract levels are important for understanding and effective intervention.
3. *Social networks* are indicated to provide buffers and supports, because people really do need people.
4. *Utilitarian resources* include money as well as tools and references that make life easier for those who have access to them than for those who do not.
5. *General and specific beliefs* influence whether people think they can master most situations or are merely victims of circumstances and include the explanations they make for occurrence of events, such as "God's will" (Folkman, Schaefer, & Lazarus, 1979).

Unfortunately, it appears that those who have the most stress (the poor and the sick), have the fewest resources (Pearlin & Schooler, 1978).

Origin of Coping Behaviors

The origin of coping behaviors is in dispute. Vaillant (Ringold, 1978) maintained that where coping behaviors come from and why one specific defense will emerge rather than some other are a great mystery. Wheaton (1980) believed internal coping resources to be learned. Consistent with this explanation is Millon's (1969) theory that coping behaviors are developed initially by trial and error, and as specific behaviors are followed by favorable results (reinforced) they are repeated. If the effectiveness continues, the behaviors are refined and become a part of the individual's behavioral repertoire. Most individuals have a wide variety of experiences with which they have had to cope and therefore have acquired some flexibility of reacting and some skill in the assessment of situations (Millon, 1969). However, the process of acquiring a repertoire of coping behaviors is greatly influenced by parents and siblings in the beginning, and then by others in the community. Aguilera and Messick (1974) pointed out that life in the cities is isolated, and this limits the availability of role models to follow. Moreover, within the ever-changing city life the coping behaviors an individual developed in the past may be ineffective against the threats in today's world.

Thus far coping behaviors have been discussed as though they were different from the defense mechanisms; however, there is support for the position that defense mechanisms are one group of coping behaviors. This would not be true if coping behaviors were defined solely as conscious processes and defense mechanisms as unconscious, but that seems to be an awkward position to maintain. Coping can be viewed as the process of meeting a threat, and the manner in which individuals commonly meet threats is by the use of defense mechanisms (Coleman, 1973). Millon (1969) contended that the intrapsychic or unconscious processes serve to take the sting out of the situation at least until the individual is capable of dealing with it realistically. The defense mechanisms make it possible for individuals to maintain some equilibrium until they can master a better solution. Lazarus (1966) agreed with this view, stating that *cop-*

ing is a general term with *defense* referring to a particular kind of coping process in which the anticipated harm is dealt with by psychological means rather than being dealt with directly (p. 28). White (1974) even questioned whether the defense mechanisms are very different from coping, because there are some continuities observed from repression to suppression, reaction formation to substitution, and rationalization to disciplined logical analysis (p. 64-65).

Defense Mechanisms

In thinking about how individuals react to difficult situations, the implication has been that the individual reacts in devious ways because of pressures from within the unconscious. This view was initiated and perpetuated by Freudian influences, and while the contribution of Freud and his followers is lauded and appreciated (White, 1974), it seems on closer observation that some, if not most, individuals are aware of the crisis situations in which they find themselves. Further, individuals make some fully conscious decisions about their subsequent behaviors. Nevertheless, the defense mechanisms—which are by definition unconscious processes—constitute an important group of coping behaviors.

Although Mechanic (1974) agreed that there are dangers in using defense mechanisms, he nevertheless emphasized that it is a serious misconception for people to assume that they must have an accurate perception of reality in order to adapt successfully. Misperceptions of reality may actually aid coping and, as Mechanic stated, such misconceptions may energize involvement and participation in life endeavors and alleviate pain and discomfort that would otherwise distract the person from successful efforts at mastery. In fact, in many of life's endeavors excessive self-awareness or introspection retards successful coping efforts (Mechanic, 1974, p. 38). The defense mechanisms, therefore, have a legitimate place among the strategies of adaptation (White, 1974, p. 64).

Although the definition of defense mechanisms varies

slightly from one writer to another, the unconscious aspect of the process is common to all the definitions. Lazarus (1966) stated that defenses are psychological maneuvers in which the individual deceives himself about the actual conditions of reality; this strategy results in the production of a benign appraisal of reality rather than a threatening one (p. 266). Others have implied that it is the subjectivity of the assessment of the environment that assists the individual in handling the stressful situation. The subjectivity applies to the distortion the individual makes of behavior as well as the distorted view of the environment (French, Rodgers, & Cobb, 1974).

Recognition of the defense mechanisms used by an individual can give the observer information as to the degree of stress the individual is experiencing (Lazarus, 1966). Often the assessment of the stress by the observer is essentially inconsequential, as it is the individual's interpretation of how personally threatening a situation is that is important. If the situation is so serious that the individual must resort to a defense mechanism as strong as denial, which seriously distorts reality, then the individual is possibly in need of some kind of therapeutic intervention. Identification of which unconscious processes an individual is using is not easy, for they must be inferred from cognitive behaviors—especially from styles of thinking and perceiving—and from discrepancies between the interpretation the individual makes and some consensual estimate of the objective circumstances (Lazarus, 1966). This difficulty in assessing the unconscious mechanisms is related to the difficulty in eliminating them. Millon (1969) pointed out that defenses are unlikely to be abandoned even if they prove maladaptive and fail to meet the individual's needs, simply because they are operating in the unconscious. The individual is unaware of the defense mechanism that is being used and is probably going to continue to use it in spite of its ineffectiveness.

Properties of Defense Mechanisms

In addition to being outside the individual's awareness, defense mechanisms are characterized by a number of properties identified by Haan (1963). The behavior associated with defense mechanisms is *rigid, stereotyped, automated,* and usually seems to be *closely associated with a particular environmental stimulus.*

> Tommy is a six-year-old who fears dogs; he always responds to the sight of an approaching dog by grabbing his mother's hand and asking to go in the opposite direction. Tommy denies his fear and perhaps even the presence of the feared stimulus by making up some excuse about changing directions.

Tommy's previous encounter of being knocked down by an overly friendly large dog seems to have an undue influence on his present behavior. This *undue influence of the past on present behavior* is another property of defense mechanisms. Note that Tommy goes to great lengths to make sure that his behavior routine remains intact in spite of the presence of small, passive dogs. A third property of defense mechanisms is the *distortion of reality,* which Tommy is exemplifying when there is no indication that the current dogs are a threat in any way. Tommy acts as though taking his mother's hand magically protects him from the dog. *Expectation of magical alleviation of the situational stress* is another property of defense mechanisms. It is unlikely that Tommy experiences any pleasure or need gratification as a result of his employing a defense mechanism for defense mechanisms are never satisfying or pleasurable. They often leave the person with vague, low-level anxiety that is rarely understood or associated with what operates it.

Categories of Defense Mechanisms

Millon (1969) divided defense mechanisms or the unconscious mechanisms, as he labeled them, into two categories: *denial mechanisms* and *distortion mechanisms*. Denial mechanisms banish intolerable memories, inpulses, and conflicts from the consciousness, while distortion mechanisms misinterpret painful thoughts and feelings in order to minimize their impact.

On the other hand, Vaillant (1971) provided a useful classification schema that ranks defense mechanisms according to their maturity. Vaillant maintained that defense mechanisms evolve as the individual matures; therefore, defenses that are appropriate for a preschooler (denial) are not always as appropriate for an adult. Obviously, some adults use denial because immature defenses may persist as a result of developmental arrest, or they may recur—in some cases appropriately—because of severe stress. In connection with his developmental approach, Vaillant emphasized the overt behavior associated with each defense, thus giving some guidance toward the identification of the defenses used by an individual and clues to their roots.

Hierarchy of Defense Mechanisms

Vaillant (1971) identified and defined four maturity levels of defenses: *narcissistic defenses, immature defenses, neurotic defenses,* and *mature defenses.* Narcissistic defense mechanisms are normal for individuals before the age of five and include delusional projection, denial, and distortion. The immature defense mechanisms are common in individuals between the ages of three and sixteen and include projection (attributing one's own unacknowledged feelings to others), schizoid fantasy, hypochondriasis, passive-aggressive behavior, and acting-out. The neurotic defense mechanisms are found in individuals throughout life beginning as early as age three. Neurotic defenses include intellectualization, repression, displacement, reaction formation, and dissociation. The mature defense mechanisms are common in healthy individuals throughout life beginning about age twelve. Mature defense mechanisms include altruism, humor, suppression, anticipation, and sublimation.

There is little consensus as to what constitutes a complete list of defense mechanisms as well as some dispute as to the definitions of the defense mechanisms. Therefore, an attempt to list the defense mechanisms in order of severity for the individual using them is preliminary at best. The degree to which the process is unconscious varies, but all defense mechanisms have an element of unconsciousness associated with them. The "healthier" ones have more conscious planning involved than do those toward the "unhealthy" end of the continuum. It should also be noted that there is overlapping among the mechanisms so that a certain behavior may fall into more than one category. Nevertheless, the defense mechanisms listed here are ordered according to seriousness of the stressful situation implied by their use by adults (because some that are healthy for children cease to be healthy when used frequently by adults). The least drastic mechanisms are defined first with progression to the most serious (see Figure 1-1).

Healthy Defense Mechanisms. Sublimation is considered to be a "healthy" defense mechanism. It represents gratification of primitive (id) needs that are unconscious and unacceptable by so-

Most Likely to be Healthy
  Sublimation
  Altruism
  Humor
  Suppression
  Anticipation
  Dissociation
  Reaction-formation
  Displacement
  Repression
  Fixation
  Regression
  Intellectualization
  Undoing
  Acting-out
  Passive-aggressive behavior
  Hypochondriasis
  Fantasy
  Compensation
  Identification
  Projection
  Distortion
  Denial
Most Likely to be Unhealthy

FIGURE 1-1. Hierarchy of adult defense mechanisms.

ciety's standards without adverse consequences or undue loss of pleasure. These needs are met by behaviors that society generally holds to be higher than the sexual drives the Freudians claim to be the basis of the underlying motivation. Aggressive needs may be met through pleasurable parlor games, sports, and hobbies. The ego is considered to be very much involved in finding acceptable channels for an individual's selfish and forbidden impulses. Instincts are channeled rather than dammed or diverted, making sublimation one of the healthier defense mechanisms. In sublimation, feelings are acknowledged, modified, and directed toward a relatively significant goal so that some instinctual gratification results (Freud, 1946; Millon, 1969; Vaillant, 1971).

Other "healthy" or "mature" defense mechanisms are altruism, humor, suppression, and anticipation. These are considered to be at the healthy end of the healthy–unhealthy continuum because they result in at least some gratification and they help an individual in coping with severely stressful situations. *Altruism* is the gaining of gratification by being of genuine service to others; the satisfaction is achieved vicariously through the knowledge of benefits one has bestowed on others. *Humor* is the overt expression of feelings but without the accompaniment of discomfort to the one doing the expressing or to others; humor makes it possible to focus on and bear that which might otherwise be unbearable. *Suppression* is the conscious or semiconscious decision to postpone thinking about something, but with suppression one remembers to think about it and handle it later. *Anticipation* is the planning for future discomforts that are realistic; such planning might include preparation for surgery, separation from a loved one, or death (Vaillant, 1971).

Unhealthy Defense Mechanisms. *Dissociation* is less healthy than the defense mechanisms just discussed. It involves the drastic, although temporary, modification of one's sense of personal identity in order to deal with what is perceived as a difficult situation. Vaillant (1971) included in this concept fugues (conditions in which individuals seem detached from their behavior); most hysterical conversion reactions (a physical manifestation of a repressed emotion); a sudden, unwarranted sense of superiority or devil-may-care attitude; short-term refusal to perceive responsibility for one's acts or feelings; overactivity and counterphobic behavior to blot out anxiety; "safe" expression of instinctual drives through acting on stage; and the use of religion or of pharmacological intoxication to numb unhappiness.

Reaction-formation is the attempt of the ego to protect itself from unacceptable urges from within by outwardly assuming a diametrically opposed opinion. This term describes the adolescent girl who "hates" the boy for whom she is feeling a physical attraction; it also encompasses crusading for a cause a person actually dislikes or protesting that one is devoted to a duty one really despises (Freud, 1946; Millon, 1969; Vaillant, 1971).

Feelings may be transferred from one object or person to another (safer) object or person through *displacement.* Frequently these feelings are negative or perceived as threatening. Displacement is seen when a man, angry with his boss for denying him a raise, avoids direct expression of the anger, but rather goes home and screams at his wife. The man denies there are negative feelings toward his boss in order to avoid confronting the boss directly, seeking other employment, or recognizing that he is not as valuable an employee as he prefers to think he is (Millon, 1969). Vaillant (1971) included practical jokes, wit with hidden and hostile intent, and caricatures as other examples of displacement.

Repression serves to get rid of instinctual drives (as opposed to threats from external stimuli) (Freud, 1946) by the simple but involuntary process of excluding one's undesirable thoughts and feelings from consciousness. This concept includes seemingly inexplicable naivete and memory lapse. The "forgetting" or repression is often accompanied by symbolic behavior indicating that the repressed material still has involuntary influence on behavior. Repression differs from suppression by affecting unconscious inhibition of drives or urges so that goals are lost rather than postponed as in suppression (Vaillant, 1971). A psychologist receives some personally tragic news just before he is to have a conference with the parents of a client.

He manages to suppress his thoughts and reaction to the news until the conference is finished and he can react privately. In contrast, a young woman thinks of her father as a warm and loving parent because she has repressed the fact that in truth he frequently beat her and her mother. Millon (1969) noted that repression is one of the most common of the defense mechanisms.

Fixation is the arrest of development or maturing at some stage, presumably due to the repression or refusal to acknowledge urges associated with a more mature developmental stage. A two-year-old who refuses to give up taking a bottle and develop appropriate autonomy is fixated in an earlier developmental stage. On the other hand, *regression* is a return or a retreat to an earlier level after having progressed to a later stage. The five-year-old who has been acting appropriately for his age until a hospitalization experience for a tonsillectomy, at which time he demands a bottle, is demonstrating regression (Millon, 1969).

Anna Freud (1946) noted that *intellectualization* is used as a precaution against the instinctual processes that are potential dangers to the individual. Thinking about instinctual wishes in a formal, affectless manner keeps the individual from having to act on those drives. Vaillant (1971) encompassed the following terms within the concept of intellectualization although he recognized differences among them: *isolation, rationalization, ritual, undoing, magical thinking,* and *busy work. Isolation* is closely related to repression and represents a limited aspect of it. When an individual uses the mechanisms of isolation, there is a separation or disconnection of what actually happened from the feelings associated with it, thus maintaining equilibrium (Millon, 1969). According to Millon, *rationalization* is the most common mechanism of reality distortion. Rationalization is an unconscious process in which a plausible explanation is given in order to mask unrecognized and unacceptable motives. *Undoing* is the process of attempting to relieve guilt of some misdeed by performing some ritualized acts. The misdeed may have been an unacceptable thought or urge as well as some overt behavior. Millon (1969) used as an illustration of undoing the example of the cutthroat businessman who donates to charity the money he has accrued by questionable means.

Acting-out, passive-aggressive behavior, and *hypochondriasis* are among the terms identified by Vaillant (1971) as "immature" defenses. He defined *acting-out* as a direct expression of an unconscious wish or impulse in order to block out awareness of the feelings accompanying it. Delinquent or impulsive behaviors, outbursts of temper, chronic use of drugs, failure, perversion, and self-inflicted injury are examples of acting-out. *Passive-aggressive behavior* is aggression toward others expressed by failure to act; it is usually masochistic and may involve turning against the self. Failure to do homework may be a child's passive-aggressive behavior toward parents. Passive-aggressive behavior is an indirect expression of feelings and is ineffective as, in the example, the parent-child conflict would not be resolved and friction would continue. *Hypochondriasis* typically occurs because of the experiences of bereavement, loneliness, or unacceptable aggressive impulses. Hypochondriasis begins with self-reproach and progresses through complaints of pain and somatic illnesses to a state of chronic and extreme fatigue (neurasthenia). This defense mechanism enables an individual to impose on others because of his pain and discomfort instead of asking for attention directly.

Sometimes individuals indulge in escape from reality by the semiconscious use of imagination to fulfill wishes that cannot be gratified in reality; this defense mechanism is *fantasy.* When fantasy involves the avoidance of interpersonal intimacy and the use of eccentricity to repel others, it has become *schizoid fantasy* (Vaillant, 1971). Although the individual does not actually believe or act on these fantasies, his or her needs for interpersonal relations are met to the point that the individual does not engage in appropriate interpersonal relationships.

Compensation is a defense mechanism whereby an individual attempts to make up for some weakness by extra efforts to overcome the weakness itself or by substituting achievement in another area. Demosthenes demonstrated such attempts as he overcame his problem of stuttering and became a well-known orator. Substituting achievement in one area to compensate for deficiencies in another is illustrated by the unattractive girl who works hard to develop her intellectual capacities to make up for her lack of good looks (Millon, 1969). In some cases compensation may be constructive, depending upon how much self-deception is involved.

Identification and projection are opposites; *identification* is a form of self-deception in which the individual attributes to himself some of the achievements and positive qualities of others, whereas *projection* is the assigning of one's undesirable and unacceptable characteristics to others. By assuming one has traits that are really not possessed, self-image is distorted (Millon, 1969). On the other hand, projection becomes quite serious when it is carried to the point of systematized delusions and acted upon (Vaillant, 1971).

Distortion is the defense mechanism whereby one reshapes the external environment to meet internal needs. According to Vaillant (1971), distortion includes unrealistic megalomaniacal beliefs, hallucinations, and wish-fulfilling delusions. For example, some students believe that they are "doing well" in their classes although objective observations would provide data indicating those students do not have sufficiently high grade point averages to remain in their programs. As compared to delusional projection, where distress is dealt with by assigning it to someone else, in distortion unpleasant feelings are replaced with their opposites. The students mentioned above would be quite happy, rather than feeling the pain of failure. This mechanism differs from reaction formation in that it is the *feeling* that is the opposite of what might be appropriate for an objective assessment of reality, rather than the *act* being the opposite of the "real" impulses. Vaillant concluded that distortion can be a highly adaptive mechanism, particularly as manifested in religious beliefs.

Millon (1969) defined denial a little differently from descriptions given by Anna Freud (1946) and Vaillant (1971). Millon included impulses and conflicts among that which is banished from consciousness, while Freud and Vaillant defined denial as the inadmission to consciousness of certain aspects of the external environment. Some denial is necessary for many of the other defense mechanisms to "work."

Use of Defense Mechanisms

The judicial use of defense mechanisms may go a long way toward relieving pain and discomfort, but as Mechanic (1974) pointed out, they may be catastrophic for personal adaptation if they reduce the use of appropriate behavior aimed at the real threats in the environment. For example, denial will do a drowning man no good. Mechanic addressed the health-related professionals in stating that the appropriate question is *when* to ease the clients into facing reality rather than *whether* it should be done. Recalling Vaillant's levels of defenses, it has been observed that the client may go through progressively more "mature" defenses as he or she moves toward functioning in the real world without self-deception.

Stress

Lazarus and Launier (1978) described stress as a very broad concept encompassing three systems: social, individual (psychological), and tissue (physiological). Stress is any event in which the environmental or internal demands (or both) tax or exceed the adaptive responses of an individual, social, or tissue system (p. 296). Wheaton (1980) noted the ambivalence as to whether stress can be defined as the stimulus, the response, or a lack of fit between stimulus and response. Appelbaum (1981) wrote that stress is an internal response to an external event (p. 10). Stress arises when there is a deviation from optimum conditions to the degree that corrective efforts are ineffective and an imbalance is created. Stress, therefore, involves an interaction between the individual and environments in which the individual interprets stimuli as harm-loss, threat, or challenge (Lazarus & Launier, 1978; Scott, Oberst, & Dropkin, 1980).

Other discussions of stress include the definition by Christman and Riehl (1974), who stated that stress is a dynamic force that produces strain or tension within the organism (p. 251). Kozier and Du Gas (1967) included the disease-producing implication in their concept of stress: "A physical, chemical or emotional factor that causes bodily or mental tension may be a factor in disease causation" (p. 20).

Selye, on the other hand, considered primarily the physiological aspects of stress and proposed that stress was a state manifested by a specific syndrome consisting of all the nonspecifically induced changes within a biologic system (1956; 1974). Bourne's (1969) approach was consistent with Selye's position: "The concept of stress has been widely accepted as a specific somatic response to damage or threat of damage by a wide variety of environmental agents, including events having a psychological rather than a physical impact" (p. 95). Millon (1969) stated that stress was a condition, either biological or psychological, that taxed the coping capacities of a person. Byrne and Thompson (1972) took a similar stand, defining stress as "a state that is always present but that is intensified when there is change or threat with which the individual must cope" (p. 42).

Since this chapter is concerned with the psychological aspects of coping, the definition proposed by Lazarus and Launier (1978) and those similar to theirs seem most appropriate for the purpose of considering stress as it relates to coping. This view considers stress to be an interaction between an environmental event and an individual who responds in order to deal with harm or loss, avoid threats, or meet challenges.

Adaptation

Adaptation is the behavior an organism uses in order to increase his chances of survival. White (1974) conceived of adaptation as a master concept incorporating the related concepts of mastery, coping, and defense. According to White, adaptation does not mean either a total triumph over the environment or total surrender to it, but rather a striving toward acceptable compromise (p. 52).

Some writers have hinted at the dangers of adaptation. Washburn, Hamburg, and Bishop (1974) conceived of adaptation as built on the past, in contrast to coping, which involves the present. If the organism depends on past adaptive behavior and fails to cope with a changing environment, it may not survive. The inability to cope has been a major contributing factor in the failure to survive of most of the extinct species (p. 7).

The term *adaptation* can mean the broad approach of the organism to survival in its environment, or it may be used as a substitute for the word *coping*. Murphy (1974) includes reflexes (built-in mechanisms), instincts (broader built-in patterns), coping efforts (to deal with situations not adequately managed by reflexes), mastery (resulting from effective and well-practiced coping efforts), and competence (the collection of skills resulting from cumulative mastery achievement) under the broader category of adaptation (p. 77).

Threat and Appraisal

Threat plays an important role in the concept of coping as indicated by Lazarus (1966); in fact, coping is a response to threat. A threat is a cognitive evaluation that one's life, health, wealth, or cherished social relationships are in danger (p. 153). Another way of defining threat is in terms of the anticipation that there is danger of interference with one's goals. The two main characteristics of threat are that it is anticipatory or future-oriented and that it is brought about by cognitive processes involving perception, learning, memory, judgment, and thought (p. 30).

Closely related to the concept of threat is the concept of appraisal, which is defined as the cognitive process that intervenes between the stimulus and the emotional reaction. Appraisal is a continuously changing set of judgments about the significance of the stimulus for the individual (Lazarus, 1966;

Lazarus, Averill, & Opton, 1970; Lazarus & Launier, 1978). Three types of appraisal are primary, secondary, and reappraisals. Primary appraisal is the process whereby the environmental stimuli are evaluated and judgment is made as to the significance of the event for the individual's well-being. A given event may be evaluated as irrelevant, benign-positive, or harmful. Secondary appraisal is the process whereby an evaluation is made of the available coping resources and options. Secondary appraisal implies that there are a number of choices usually available from which people can select the "best." The choices may be to engage, flee, or seek relief in some defense mechanism. Reappraisal refers to a feedback system in which appraisals are expanded to include information from one's own reaction and from the environment.

Lazarus (1966) argued that the concept of threat is a better unifying term for all of the affective reactions than the traditional concepts of anxiety or fear. The problem with using the term *anxiety* is that it refers to only one affect, and this limits it. When an individual is *threatened* he or she may be anxious, frightened, angry, depressed, or experience any of the other affective reactions. All of these different patterns of reaction involve the underlying condition of threat (p. 74).

Crisis

The various definitions of crisis have several elements in common: (a) the concept of change or occurrence of new challenges; (b) the concept that coping behaviors used in the past are no longer effective even though how people meet a crisis is determined by their past history; and (c) the concept that successful resolution of the crisis provides potential for personal growth and maturity whereas unsuccessful resolution or lack of resolution of the crisis has potential for emotional or physical illness. The new threats may be environmental, such as loss of a loved one or loss of property by fire or flood, or internal, such as puberty or menopause.

Pittman (in Langsley & Kaplan, 1968) defined crisis as a

state of readiness for change and stated that it is not necessarily an emergency. According to Adams and Lindemann (1974) the critical issues concern the choice of adaptive patterns, for these patterns may be predominantly regressive and defensive, functioning primarily for the protection of the self from disintegration, or they may represent efforts to master the environment, restructure the task ahead, and solve the problems of dealing with a novel situation (p. 128). The feeling of helplessness experienced by some people faced with a crisis is included in the definition by Aguilera and Messick (1974), who noted that such people feel caught in a state of great emotional upset and may believe themselves unable to solve their problems alone (p. 1).

By definition, then, a crisis is a new situation involving novel internal and external forces. Caplan (1964) observed that chance plays a part in the outcome of a crisis along with the bodily state of the individual at the time, the availability of support from significant others, the environmental communication system, and the personality of the individual (p. 41).

Mastery

Mastery implies the achievement of some standard. Looking back to the definition of adaptation, mastery is one aspect of adaptation achieved as the result of successful coping efforts. As such, mastery includes learning to deal comfortably and perhaps routinely with some element of the environment, for example, mastering the task of walking on an artificial leg or, developmentally, the infant's mastery of walking. Mastery is the result of effective and well-practiced coping efforts (French, Rodgers & Cobb, 1974; Lazarus, 1966; Murphy, 1974).

Resilience

Resilience, although not frequently described in the literature, is encountered in working with clients. Resilience is a quality to seek and reinforce. Perhaps it is because of her work with children that Lois Murphy has emphasized the concept of resilience, since it is a quality that is often well-exemplified in children. Murphy (1974) defined resilience as an active psychophysiological push to restore a satisfying state of being as the individual is shifted from pain to pleasure or from disturbance to comfort. The individual must have the physiological capacity for self-healing. The goal of resilience is to resolve disruptions in functioning and return to optimal levels (p. 96). An example of resilience follows:

> Tommy, a five-year-old boy, has been in six foster homes in the past seven months. He is always sad about leaving a home and extremely tearful when an anticipated weekend with his "real" mother is thwarted, but so far he has managed to "bounce back," repeat the words of the protective service worker that his mother is "all right," and look forward to seeing his little brother or grandmother.

Adjustment

Like resilience, adjustment is often an overlooked but important term. French, Rodgers, and Cobb (1974) provided a useful distinction between the objective and subjective persons and environments as they pertain to adjustment. Adjustment is defined as the goodness of fit between the characteristics of the person and the properties of the environment. The objective environment is that which exists independently of the person's perception of it, and the subjective environment is that which is perceived and reported by the person. Likewise, there are the persons as they really are (the objective persons) and the persons as they conceive of themselves (the subjective persons). The implication is that there are at least two conceptions of adjustment: the objective fit between the objective person and the objective environment and the subjective fit between the subjective person and the subjective environment. The psychotic individual may be adjusting perfectly in terms of how the subjective self is functioning in the subjective environment, but the objective self will be behaving inappropriately according to observers of the individual and his objective environment.

SUMMARY

In summary of how the other terms discussed in this chapter relate to the concept of coping, adaptation was defined as a master concept that has survival as its goal; coping behaviors are used as one type of weapon in the arsenal of instruments for survival (see Figure 1-2). Stress and threat are factors that are potentially harmful to the individual and are identified by appraisal. After identifying environmental cues as potentially threatening, secondary appraisal occurs, in which the individual evaluates the available coping behaviors and chooses the one

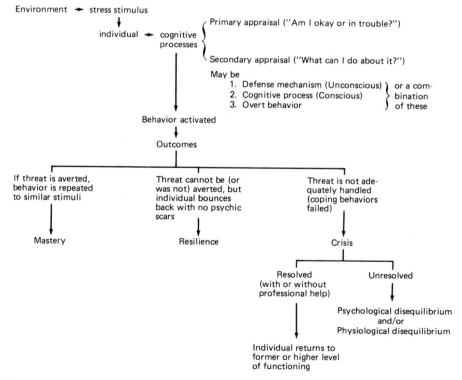

FIGURE 1-2. Adaptation. (A change in adaptation may indicate adjustment.)

that would appear to be best for the present situation. A crisis is a potentially threatening situation that calls for the mobilization of coping behaviors. Individuals who use coping behaviors appropriately and repeatedly to meet a particular type of threat until the behaviors are employed automatically and perhaps unconsciously have reached a level of mastery. When an individual uses appropriate coping behaviors repeatedly in various situations and continues to bounce back to a state of equilibrium, he or she is exhibiting resilience.

Adjustment means "fitting in"; fitting into one's society was the goal of adolescents as they set upon their quest for identity, according to Erikson's (1950) formulation of life's developmental crises. However, in present times the task has shifted away from learning to adjust, for that would make the individual obsolete by the time he or she had accomplished it. Instead, today's adolescent must learn to cope.

> Coping involves emphasis on internal balance and lacks the aspects of concession implied by the term "adjustment." Furthermore, coping implies realistic perception and awareness with a minimum of ideological interpretation and hence, distortion. Depending on the limitations inner realities place on persòns, their coping efforts allow them to deal appropriately with reality without making concessions. (Moriarty & Toussieng, 1976, p. 141)

Although coping is only one aspect of adaptation, it is believed to be a vital aspect and a process that has challenging implications for health-related professionals. Health-related professionals become involved with individuals at the time when the individuals are in a state of readiness for change. Change, however, is always resisted to some degree. (Even highly desired changes such as marriages, births, or promotions are met with some ambivalence that includes resistance.) Clients in health maintenance clinics or primary prevention situations as well as clients in acute care settings are experiencing at least external pressure to change. The internal resistance may contribute to the inappropriate choice of a coping behavior or to the misapplication of the coping strategy to the client's situation. In crisis, the individual must employ some coping behaviors; it is at that time that the helper has the opportunity to evaluate whether the coping behaviors the individual is using are appropriate. If the behaviors are appropriate, the helper can support the client in the use of them, or if not the helper can suggest other coping behaviors and help the client learn to use them. Discussion will be focused on this aspect of intervention in Chapter 4.

Chapter 2

The Primary Biophysical-Psychosocial Influences of Behavior

Individual behavior development depends on the interaction of structure, function, and the milieu (internal and external environment). Among the variables that influence the uniqueness of individual behavior are the coping responses. Therefore, an overview of primary biophysical-psychosocial development will provide a general background for understanding the development and effects of coping responses in our clients and ourselves as care providers.

OVERVIEW

Each individual species has complex patterns of activities that enable its members to maintain and continue the life processes, including biological, procreative, and social functions. In addition, the human organism surpasses other species in the resources essential for flexibility and manipulatory activity within the environment. This ability is the result of the almost infinite capability of the human being to generate, test, modify, store, and exchange ideas and information. These attributes are possible because of the intricate development of the sophisticated central and peripheral nervous system, designed to interact appropriately with the internal and external environment unless a deviation exists.

In an open system, where energy flows between an organism and its environment, the intake of matter must be adequate to provide sufficient energy for the organism to maintain itself in a state of balance within the environment. All components of the organism possess the genetic materials essential for their particular structure and function. For example, the genetic code of the organism will determine that a particular organ will consist of cells and tissues that will form the kidney—and that nerve cells will differ from it in form and function. The cell, which is the primary machinery of physiologic function, consists of cytoplasm and functional organelles. Basic compounds in cells include water, proteins, and other regulative organic and inorganic compounds.

The brain, spinal cord, and peripheral nerves provide the

integrating control for the entire organism via hormonal and chemical transmitters. Kolb (1977) identified the functions of three critical subsystems of the organism influenced by this control as follows. The first subsystem is concerned with the processing of information registered upon the body from its interior and exterior surfaces, its organ systems, and its own structures. For example, the epidermal-dermal layers of the skin protect the underlying structures but also respond to touch and pressure stimuli. A second subsystem processes matter energy through the physiological activities of respiration, feeding, drinking, and elimination of carbon dioxide, fecal matter, and urine. The third subsystem includes the physiological and psychological functions that enable the species to reproduce itself.

To summarize the integrating control activities, the brain receives varied inputs from the environment that must be processed, including the work of the subsystem responsible for matter-energy and the subsystem related to survival, that is, information-processing (Kolb, 1977). The information input comes from receptors; is transferred through supersensitive networks to decoders; and is stored for long or short terms with previously acquired information or relayed on cue to the output component of the subsystem. This process ensures that the requisite behavior maintains and reaffirms balance within the system.

Feedback mechanisms influence the processing of internal and external input into the system in order to modify stress. The feedback network for the individual not only includes the physiological environment, but extends to the individual's psychosocial relationships within the hierarchy of complex social suprasystems, that is, the family or surrogates and the range of supportive or challenging parts of the institutions that affect the individual. These structured and unstructured interactions in the hierarchy enable the individual to develop a distinctive personality, test this development against the normative behavior in society, and modify personal behavior and the social suprasystem (Brim, 1960; Brim & Wheeler, 1966).

In essence, the behavior of the individual is generated through a complex series of biophysical and psychosocial interactions, including the influences of maturation, genetic potential, health states (physiological and psychological), exposure and responsiveness to stimuli, and the range of the previously learned behavior stored as memory. Some of the salient generators of human behavior are included in the following discussion.

THE BIOPHYSICAL ASPECTS

Nervous System Regulation and Overview

The nervous system of an individual is a complex regulatory subsystem that has evolved into a primary communication network capable of the coordination of functions of all body systems. The nervous system enables the human organism to learn, reason, dream, relate, filter, project, and plan through complex communications (Kolb, 1977). Component cells of this network are minute electrochemical units capable of responding to stimuli.

Response is seldom a simple, discrete operation, however. It depends upon the nature of the stimulus, the storage of information available from previously learned events, the hormonal influences, and the state of the pathways. To perform at the baseline level, these pathways of the nervous system must be functional. If they are not functional, aberrations occur, with possible unsatisfactory compensations of the input-output system of the individual.

The Peripheral and Autonomic Nervous Systems as Integrators of Control

The peripheral nervous system (PNS) consists of all nerve cells that lie outside of the skull or the vertebral column. This system includes the autonomic nervous system (ANS) as well as the cranial nerves and their dorsal and ventral roots and the peripheral branches. The peripheral nerves arise from plexuses formed by spinal nerves (Figure 2-1). The cranial nerves arise

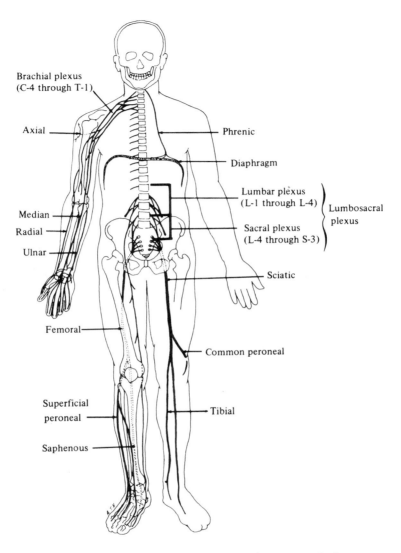

Brachial plexus
(C-4 through T-1)

Axial

Phrenic

Diaphragm

Median

Radial

Ulnar

Lumbar plexus
(L-1 through L-4)

Sacral plexus
(L-4 through S-3)

Lumbosacral
plexus

Sciatic

Femoral

Common peroneal

Superficial
peroneal

Tibial

Saphenous

FIGURE 2-1. Anterior view of peripheral nerves and plexuses. [Adapted from Ellen E. Chaffee and Esther M. Greisheimer, *Basic Physiology and Anatomy*, 3rd edition (Philadelphia: J.B. Lippincott, 1974)]

along the length of the spinal cord and carry both sensory and motor fibers. Sensory fibers arise in the periphery from specialized processes close to or attached to a receptor. Impulses arising when the receptors are stimulated are transmitted toward the cord to the cell body in the dorsal root of the spinal

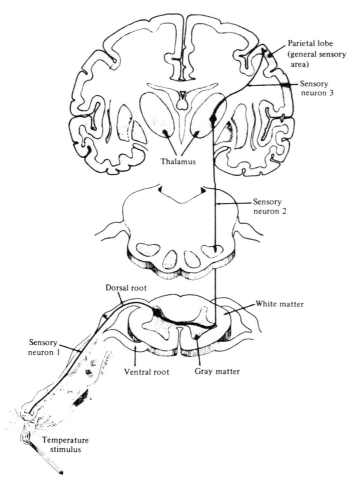

FIGURE 2-2. Sensory impulse pathway. Sensory impulses cross over to the opposite side of the cord from which they originate. They travel over three neurons to the sensory area of the cerebral cortex.

nerve, and from there the information is passed on to the adjacent cells. Motor nerves transmit impulses from the cord to the effector organs. In the cranial nerve subsystem, sensory nerves transmit impulses to the brain and motor nerves transmit impulses from the brain to the effector organs (see Figure 2-2).

Ganglia are collections of the neuronal cell bodies located outside of the central nervous system (CNS) (see Figure 2-3). Spinal nerves leave the spinal column from the level of the cervical to the lumbar spine. The sensory and motor pathways extend from the second lumbar vertebra to the foramen magnum, which is protected by the skull. The autonomic nervous system is a division of the PNS and innervates smooth muscle and the cardiac muscle and glands.

Chemical Transmitters

Certain synaptic functions must occur in order for this system to transmit information (see Figure 2-4). The synapse itself is the point at which the axon abuts on the next neuron. Along the surfaces of the dendrites and soma are hundreds of tiny synaptic knobs. These synaptic knobs are located on the terminal ends of the nerve fibrils of autonomic fibers. The synapses are excitatory or inhibitory, dependent upon the particular secretory chemical substance of their vesicles. Adenosine triphosphate (ATP), the synthesizing activator, is located in the mitochondria of the knob. The chemical substances, or transmitters (Figure 2-5), are synthesized rapidly because the stored amounts in the vesicles are sufficient only for very brief time spans (a few seconds to a few minutes) of maximum activity. However, the process of synthesis is continuous (Guyton, 1976).

It is the spread of the action potential that causes membranes to depolarize and a number of vesicles to empty into the synaptic cleft (between the presynaptic terminal and postsynaptic receptor area in the soma of the neuron). This action produces a change in the permeability of the subsynaptic neuronal membrane. The excitatory or inhibitory response, as noted previously, is dependent upon the chemical transmitter.

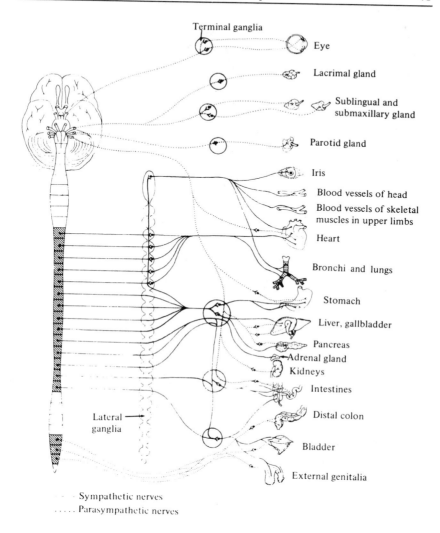

FIGURE 2-3. Sympathetic and parasympathetic nerves and the organs and tissues they innervate.

Although some of the process of this change is hypothesized at present, preliminary findings demonstrate that a decrease in the calcium and sodium ions reduces the number of vesicles released with each action potential. However, an increase in the magnesium ions or partial depolarization of the membrane oc-

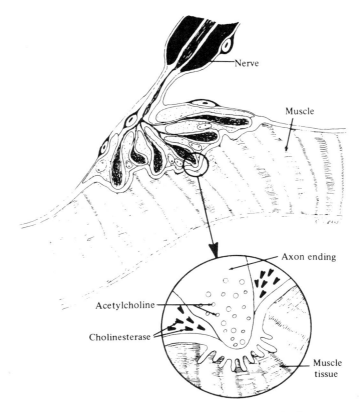

FIGURE 2-4. Myoneural junction. A nerve impulse is transmitted from neurons to muscle tissue by neurotransmitters, such as acetylcholine. Acetylcholine acts to depolarize the muscle tissue and thereby initiate a nerve impulse.

curring prior to the transmission of the action potential weakens the potential.

The chemical transmitter action hypothesis states that the site of the synaptic knob abutment contains specific receptor molecules that bind the transmitter substance. The receptors may be proteins that respond to the chemical transmitters through changes in shape or action in order to increase permeability. For example, the membrane permeability to sodium ions increases if the transmitter is excitatory or the permeability

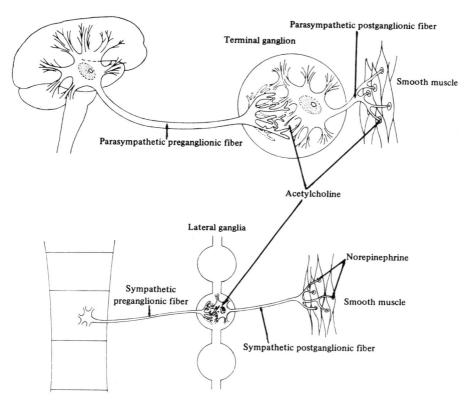

FIGURE 2-5. Chemical transmitters released by sympathetic and parasympathetic neurons. Notice that acetylcholine is released by preganglionic neurons of the parasympathetic and sympathetic systems as well as the postganglionic neurons of the parasympathetic system. The postganglionic neurons of the sympathetic system release norepinephrine.

to chloride ions and potassium increases if the transmitter is inhibitory. Guyton (1976) stated that a "memory function" may enable the postsynaptic receptor area to increase with the intensity of the synapse activity because the ribosomes and endoplasmic reticulum increased beneath the synapse itself.

Examples of excitatory chemical transmitters include granules of acetylcholine, norepinephrine, dopamine, and serotonin. Acetylcholine, choline acetyl transferase (needed for the acetyl choline synthesis) and cholinesteras (needed for splitting acetylcholine after secretion) are released from different types of synaptic knobs found in widespread areas of the nervous system (Guyton, 1976). The action of acetylcholine, which transmits between pre- and postganglionic fibers in parasympathetic and sympathetic systems, stimulates neuron or muscle fibers. Norepinephrine, which transmits between sympathetic postganglionic fibers, stimulates cardiac and some smooth muscle fibers. Dopamine and norepinephrine affect the blood vessels through vasoconstriction and are associated with subjective or elevated mood in an individual. That is, they increase activity and enhance rage behavior. Serotonin is found in the chromaffin tissue of the intestine and abdominal organs as well as in the platelets. The effects of serotonin vary from vasodilation to constriction of blood vessels, depending on the state of the circulation at the time of stimulation. As a consequence of this variation dependent on circulation and other physiological variables, serotonin may dampen aggressive drives and control impulses in the individual—or it may increase the development of angry behavior.

Inhibitory chemical transmitters include gamma aminobutyric acid (GABA) and glycine. GABA is more plentiful in brain nerve terminals than in the spinal cord. Its action has been documented in some lower animals; therefore, it is assumed that it acts in mammals. Glycine is a simple amino acid that is present in a highly concentrated form in some spinal cord synaptic knobs and is reported to be an inhibitory transmitter in those synapses.

Other newly recognized substances that are possible transmitters include L-glutamate and L-asparate as excitatory transmitters and taurine and alanine as inhibitory transmitters, as well as histamine, prostaglandins, and P-substances (polypeptides found in the nervous system), which may have prolonged excitatory or inhibitory effects on neurons. The excitatory and inhibitory chemical transmitters affect the vast neural network in ways that influence learning (Vander, Sherman & Luciano, 1980).

Levels of Nervous Control

The cerebral cortex, hypothalamus, brain stem, spinal cord, and ganglia comprise the levels of nervous control in the ANS. At the lower levels of control, the functions and connections are less general, more constricted, and specific, whereas the reverse occurs at the upper levels of control. Preganglionic fibers from the CNS synapse with peripherally located ganglion cells and arrive at the viscera as postganglionic fibers. The axons from oculomotor, facial, glossopharyngeal, vagus, and accessory nerves comprise the cranial sacral or parasympathetic division. The axons that leave by the ventral roots of the thorax and the first three lumbar roots form the sympathetic system. Ganglia are located in, or adjacent to, innervated organs, and paravertebral and prevertebral ganglia are the peripheral sites of the peripheral synapses.

Research studies demonstrate that the hypothalamus performs visceral and metabolic functions by its effects on the brain stem and the hypophysis, thereby acting on the endocrine system and the nerve network. Visceral responses influenced by the brain stem include the reflex control of blood pressure and respiration, as well as influences on the peripheral autonomic ganglia, the lowest and most specific autonomic ganglia (Gardner, 1968). The parasympathetic nervous system is responsible for the regulation of the more specific functions of the body, including functions of the gastrointestinal and urinary systems, in response to rather specific stimuli.

Summary of the ANS

In summary, the ANS is a voluntary and involuntary system. Through the voluntary function, it enables the human organism to perform consciously, engage in mental pursuits, and perform precise, deliberate activities. The involuntary function enables the processes to occur that are independent, not within the awareness level, and unconsciously controlled. For example, the regulation of heartbeat, blood pressure, respiration and digestion, and the influence of the feedback mechanisms that permit variations to occur in the stressful state followed by compensations and restoration of normalcy are largely involuntary functions (Pansky, 1975). The sympathetic subsystem, then, regulates the responses needed for action such as increased respiratory rate, heart rate, and the glucose mobilization and increased oxygenation required for muscle use. The parasympathetic subsystem performs as a counterbalance to the sympathetic regulation and influences the restoration of normalcy after stress. It prepares the body for further efforts and responds to more specific stimuli. Either system may be excitatory, as the sympathetic subsystem can vasodilate the coronary arteries but vasoconstrict the arteries of the head. Anatomically, the system is comprised of motor nerves that differ from other peripheral nerves in that the neuron leaves the CNS and links with another whose cells are located in ganglia instead of the effector organ (Pansky, 1975). Thus, this nervous system complex is responsible for receiving information through different impulses; relaying the information appropriately through its subsystems of interconnections and relays; and transmitting the information through efferent impulses.

The Brainstem

The next higher structure is a component within the central nervous system, the brainstem. It is composed of the thalamus and hypothalamus, midbrain, pons, and medulla (Figure 2-6). The connections to the cerebral hemispheres (higher brain) from this component are through the internal capsule to the cerebellum by way of the three paired cerebellar fiber bundles, the superior, middle, and inferior peduncles. The several parts have discrete as well as collaborative integrating functions and the primary ones are noted here.

The thalamus functions as a center for receiving impulses from ascending, associating, and some descending fibers. It correlates, integrates, and distributes impulses to specific areas of the cerebral cortex, basal nuclei, hypothalamus, cerebellum,

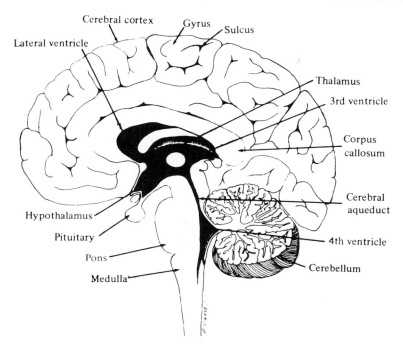

FIGURE 2-6. Sagittal view of brain.

and other nuclei of the brainstem. It contributes to the awareness and consciousness state, influences voluntary movements,
and responds to cerebral stimuli.

The hypothalamus regulates the sympathetic and parasympathetic components of the CNS through the cardiovascular
and respiratory centers of the medulla, the body temperature
through vasodilation and vasoconstriction, and the appetite by
subtle changes in the carbohydrate concentration in blood
plasma and stomach distention. Through the pituitary gland,
the hypothalamus influences the endocrine activities related to
lactation, ovulation, puberty onset, menstrual cycle, water balance, and patterns of growth and development. With the reticular activating system (RAS), the hypothalamus influences
the awareness state; thus this particular function of the hypothalamus is important in any explanation of behavior.

The Reticular Activating System (RAS)

Livanov (1962) used the toposcope to demonstrate by electro-physiological methods that points of optimal excitation in the cortex of the brain of an animal could be identified. This finding enabled subsequent investigations to follow the televised cortical responses from excitation to extinguishment. Additional study indicated that an optimal level of cortical tone is necessary for organized mental responses to occur. Learning and related meaningful behavior, then, depend highly on a subsystem designed for maintenance and regulatory control of cortical tone. This subsystem is not located in the cortex itself, but in the subcortex and brainstem (Luria, 1973). These structures not only influence the cortical tone but experience the regulatory influence themselves (Magoun, 1963). This brainstem nerve tissue, the RAS (Figure 2-7), has special morphological structure and functional properties consisting of a nerve net with scattered nerve cells that regulate the cerebral cortical state. In

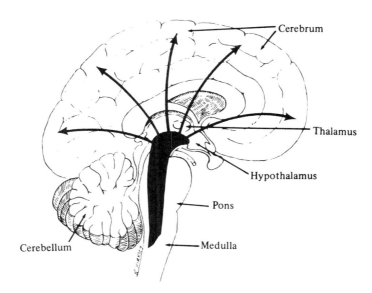

FIGURE 2-7. The reticular activating system is shown sending impulses to the various areas of the brain.

summary, the stimulus from the receptors moves gradually over the net of the RAS instead of along isolated neurons that produce excitation in an "all or none" fashion (Luria, 1973). This gradual movement of the stimulus alters the level of excitation little by little, thereby modulating the state of receptivity of the nervous system.

The fibers of the RAS that extend to the thalamus, caudate body, archicortex, and neocortex are components of the ascending reticular system (ARS). The primary ARS function is to activate and regulate the cortex. Fibers that begin in the neocortex and archicortex, caudate body, and the thalamic nuclei components of the descending reticular system (DRS) extend to the lower structures in the mesencephalon, hypothalamus, and brainstem. The action of this net subordinates the lower structures to the control of cortical programs wherein modification and modulation of the waking state are essential.

Studies of reticular formation and response from the last three decades, testing the principles of vertical organization and hierarchical relationships of the brain structures, expanded the research and treatment possibilities for the problems of the human organism. This broadened base emphasized the power of the reticular formation as a mechanism for the maintenance of cortical tone, for regulation of the functional state of the brain, and as a primary determiner of the level of wakefulness and inhibition in the individual (Luria, 1973). Further, this net was observed to have the power to differentiate and specify cortical excitation through metabolic processes (the internal economy), through the orienting reflex (the mobilization needed for adjustment to the environmental changes), and through mechanisms for conscious social interaction (speech). The RAS, then, has a major function in the influence of the behavior of the human organism.

The Cortex and Its Subsystems

The cerbral cortex and its subsystems (Figure 2-8) comprise the outer portion of the cerebral hemispheres. This structure con-

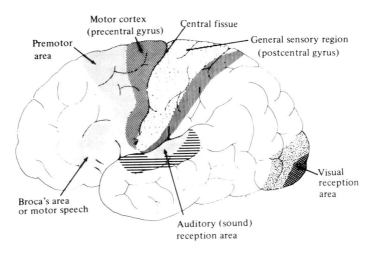

FIGURE 2-8. Lateral view of functional areas in the lobes of cerebral cortex.

sists of several lobes or parts, including frontal, occipital, parietal, and temporal, which are primarily stimulus specific. That is, particular neurons, when stimulated, lead to specific activity (Vander, et al., 1980). This vast unit receives, analyzes, and stores information by receiving and relaying impulses to groups of neurons that respond in the "all or none" fashion, as contrasted to the RAS mode of gradualism. These neurons (primarily of afferent layer IV) are often extremely specific in that they are responsive to highly specialized properties of stimuli. The neurons of the cortical visual system are an example. However, the unit does contain some multimodal cells that respond to several types of stimuli (Luria, 1973).

The cortex and related visual, auditory, and parietal (general sensory) subsystems contribute to the human gnostic or "knowing" activity through complex processes that transmit the stimuli to the appropriate cortical ends of the analyzers. These analyzers overlap in the zones located on the boundaries between the occipital, temporal, and postcentral cortex. The largest area of concentration is located in the inferior parietal region, one that achieved a considerable size in the process of human evolutional development (Luria, 1973). These zones influence spatial organization, thereby integrating information from the specific system (e.g., visual) and transfer the information from the direct representation to a level of symbolism. This internal process provides for the conversion of concrete perceptions into abstractions. The process also provides for the organization and storage of experience in memory to occur, the reception, coding, and storage detail (Luria, 1973).

The anterior regions of the hemispheres anterior to the precentral gyrus are responsible for programming, regulating, and verifying conscious activity. The motor cortex (Brodmann's area IV) is the outlet channel, which contains the giant pyramidal cells of Betz (Luria, 1973). The fibers run from the spinal motor nuclei to the muscles, thereby forming the parts of the great pyramidal tract. Fibers leading to the lower limbs originate in the superior parts; fibers leading to the upper limbs of the contralateral side originate in the medial fiber parts; and fibers extending to the facial, lip, and tongue areas originate in the lower portions of the tract. The motor impulses, however, do not function totally as pyramidal cell responses, but depend upon the preparation of motor programs from secondary areas of the motor cortex and the precentral gyrus. The upper layers of the cortex and the extracellular grey matter elements (dendrites and glia) assist in the preparation of the motor programs and in their transmission to the pyramidal cells (Luria, 1973). The human organism has a high index of extracellular grey matter in proportion to that of lower primates, indicative of the refinement of this structure (Bonin, 1943; 1948) and the potential for the wide range of behavior in the species.

The premotor areas, then, possess the powers needed for organization relative to the movement of individual muscles as well as the more systematic organized movements of structures in the body such as head turning, hand grasping, or even total body movement. These processes are accomplished through efferent motor systems under afferent control. Of note also is the validation of the "principle of widest representation," which means that organs that have the greatest value and/or require the keenest regulation have priority in the "regulatory priority."

Of utmost importance in the frontal region of the brain itself is the granular frontal cortex, a region that does not contain pyramidal cells. It has a function in the formation of plans and programs and in the regulation and verification of complex human behavior. This function is accomplished through connections to the medial and ventral nuclei and the pulvinar of the thalamus, and with other RAS structures and almost all parts of the cortex. This network facilitates the reception and synthesis of afferent impulses from the diverse parts of the brain. It also permits the organization of efferent impulses to regulate the structure involved. Medial and basal portions of the frontal lobes are connected with the reticular formation by bundles of ascending and descending fibers. These parts receive impulses from the reticular net, where they are energized or modulated in order for the impulses to conform to a scheme of behavior formed with the frontal cortex.

The prefrontal cortex is a suprasystem. Through its medial and basal components it influences and regulates the state of activity. It changes the activity to meet the individual's plans and intentions formed with the consciousness of speech, thereby enabling the organization and goal direction of human behavior to occur. Of note is the fact that most of the physical development of the prefrontal cortex occurs late ontologically, that is, the cortex of a child achieves its proportionate size between four and seven years of age (Luria, 1961; 1969). This is a partial explanation for the dominance of concrete over abstract representation in the thought processes of younger children.

Finally, the frontal lobes function not only in the organization and goal direction of behavior, but also in the so-called reflexive response of the reflex arc. Anokhin (1935) and others expanded the arc concept to "reflex ring" or "circle" because the reception and analysis of stimuli from the external milieu and the response to them require a consideration of the effects of the action on the brain of the individual. This "reverse afferentation" on "action acceptor" apparatus makes organized action possible through the frontal lobe activity. This activity includes the synthesis of external stimuli as preparation for the effect of the response and the verification that the response has transpired properly to occur (Luria, 1973; Pribram, 1961).

Speech as a cortical function (programming, relating, and verifying the performance) of the human brain reflects almost all of the higher mental processes and conscious activity, including contrasting, differentiating and decision-making. Further, although each element noted is a complex functional system, speech is also a consequence of the action of several units of the brain. That is, mental functions are not isolated faculties that are localized in particular brain sites. The model for mental processes congruent with this theory consists of a self-regulating system, a reflex ring, with each component containing afferent and effector elements (Leontiev, 1959). For example, perception is a consequence of the requisite cortical tone, an analysis and synthesis of the information received, and the characteristic searching movements.

Neuroendocrine System Regulation

Although the relationship between the neurological and endocrine systems has been discussed, a more detailed review of the neuroendocrine-effector organ response is necessary for understanding the concept of the physiology of stress. Regardless of the classification of stress—physiological or psychosocial, specific or nonspecific—the physiological response of the body shows characteristic patterns through hormonal and nervous stimulation and their effects on the target organs.

In the response to a stressor, the hypothalamus at the base of the brain, with connections to nuclei of the cerebral hemispheres and brainstem, produces an ACTH-releasing factor that causes the hypophysis of the pituitary gland to increase ACTH secretion (the adrenocorticotrophic hormone), which stimulates the adrenal cortex to enlarge and increase the production of the glucocorticoids (e.g., cortisone). This substance stimulates thymus and lymph node involution and the organic metabolism of glucose. With this corticoid stimulation, the corticoid-containing lipid storage material diminishes and compensatory hemoconcentration, hypochloremia, and general tissue catabolism occurs with an overall decrease in body weight of the individual. Concurrently, the stressor activates the autonomic nervous system and initiates the gastrointestinal effector organ system response, an organ system simultaneously stimulated by adrenal secretions. As an autonomic response, the medulla of the adrenals secretes epinephrine and norepinephrine, and the synapses of the sympathetic preganglionic neurons also secrete norepinephrine under the control of the thoracolumbar division of the parasympathetic division of the ANS. This response is inherent to the "fight or flight" action in which the smooth muscle blood supply is sacrificed for the more striated muscle supply needed for the so-called survival action (Cannon, 1939). The heart and respiratory rate may increase (dependent upon the time interval since a meal), and the electrolytes, particularly potassium and magnesium, may diminish in the blood. Also, the immunosuppressive and phagocytic mechanism is active in antibody formation, as part of the reticulo-endothelial system responsiveness during stress.

STRESS THEORY

Although they are occasionally used interchangeably, the concepts of *stress* and *stressors* differ. Selye (1973) defined stress as the nonspecific response of the body to any demand made upon it. The stress-producer is the stressor. It may have the form of a pleasant or unpleasant situation or innocuous or noxious element, but its importance—physiological and psychological—rests in the intensity of its demand for a change, for a readjustment or adaptation.

The example Selye presented depicts two specific events, one pleasant and the other unpleasant. The stressors in the example differ in that in one event a mother learns that her son died in battle and she suffers an extreme mental shock; later, the mother learns that her son is alive and she experiences great joy. In each event, the mother's overt response to the stressor is different, but the demand for an adjustment to the stressor may have been the same. The demand requires that the individual adapt to the problem or stress created by the stressor. The stress in the illustration produced a need for the mother to perform particular adaptive functions and regain her state of normalcy. This demand on the body, stated Selye, comprises the "essence of stress." The stressor effect depends solely on the intensity of the demand made upon the adaptive function of the body—not its damage.

Lazarus (1966) distinguished between physiological and psychological stress in that the former is a response to a physical damage already incurred whereas the latter is a response to psychological harm anticipated from cues that are interpreted as portending harm. Millon (1969) stated that the biological or psychological condition that taxes the coping capacities of a person is stress.

Selye (1973) has not dwelled on the differences between psychological and physiological stress. His work has followed and supported the early work of Cannon (1938) and subsequent physiologists, who demonstrated by objective quantitative biochemical determination that a range of emotional arousers as well as physical stressors produce particular physiological reactions of the body that are both nonspecific and common to all types of stress. The stressors identified include heat, cold, biochemicals, hormones, microorganisms, foods, and drugs. Further, these studies indicated that stressors produce stress reactions in lower animals, in those without nervous systems, and in plants.

General Adaptation Syndrome (GAS)

The prominent Selye theory pertaining to the manner in which the body responds to stress was presented in 1936. Selye described an often observed syndrome, the response of the individual to noxious agents. Later, the general response was identified as the "general adaptation syndrome" (GAS).

The three stages of this general response consist of the alarm reaction, the stage of resistance, and the stage of exhaustion. Descriptions of the stages, including the physiological reactions, are summarized here in order to clarify the concept of physiological adaptation, its antecedent, and the outcome state if heterostasis/homeostasis (wherein homeostasis is raised artificially to a higher level through the use of natural or exogenous elements) is not achieved.

The two phases of the alarm reaction are the shock and countershock, wherein the body responds to injury with catabolic changes and subsequently is restored to the preinjury state. The characteristic alarm reaction includes the adrenal cortical discharge of secretory granules into the bloodstream, thereby depleting the corticoid-containing lipid storage material. Subsequently, hemoconcentration, hypochloremia, and general catabolism of the tissue occurs. These responses affect the general response as well as modifying the local response to the insult. The type of local change is dependent upon which adrenocortical hormones predominate (Selye, 1973). Thus, the mineralocorticoids are needed to stimulate connective tissue to develop and to influence the inflammatory response, whereas the glucocorticoids are anti-inflammatory in order to suppress or control the inflammatory process and reduce the scar tissue formation. In the stage of resistance, the adrenal cortex again has a rich store of the secretory granules and hemodilution, hyperchloremia, and the return of the individual to normal weight occurs as a consequence of anabolism. This adaptive stage enables the individual to respond through three distinct mechanisms. Selye identified these as the nervous, immunologic and phagocytic, and hormonal mechanisms. A brief description of these mechanisms follows.

In the nervous mechanism, the individual may consciously plan a defense (e.g., decide to fight or flee) and/or produce action through his or her reflex system (innate *or* conditioned) and the autonomic nervous system through the assistance of the neurohormonal responses (the initiation of the flight or flee response). The immunologic and phagocytic mechanism activates the antibody formation and the recticuloendothelial system in order to resist the invasion of "alien elements" such as microbes, abnormal proteins or other agents, and organ transplants and grafts.

The hormonal mechanism functions through syntoxic hormones (those that serve to tranquilize the tissue) in order to allow the body to tolerate the invader or pathogen without attacking it directly. The glucocorticoids prevent inflammation but do not destroy it. In addition, catatoxic substances (those that produce chemical changes largely through the production of destructive enzymes) eliminate the aggressive agent. For example, those steroids and drugs that hasten biodegradation of toxic elements without promoting the resistance of tissue to them are catatoxic (Selye, 1971). With continued exposure to the stressor, the compensation and acquired adaptation of the stage of resistance diminish and the stage of exhaustion occurs. The stage of exhaustion is inevitable, according to the theory, when the stressor is severe and its duration is for a sufficient time. This indicates that adaptation of the body is finite. This stage (shock), if it is not interrupted appropriately, leads to death.

Mason (1971, 1975), however, demonstrated in his work with primates that several neuroendocrine axes influence the restoration of balance in the presence of particular stressors and that the patterns of hormonal excretions varied with each of four stressors tested. Although the multiple endocrine secretory effects were similar to the effects attributed to the general arousal response proposed by Selye, Mason reported that each of the stressors of heat, cold, hunger, and exercise produced different patterns of hormonal secretion, supportive of a theory of specific adaptational response.

Adaptation, by implication, is an important characteristic of life, dependent on a range of responses: nervous, immunologic, phagocytic, or hormonal mediation. Adaptation can lead to the healthy state of homeostasis/heterostasis, or maladaptation ultimately can lead to death of the individual. However, the complexities of the compensatory mechanisms and the range of any behavior, physiological or psychological, enable maladaptation to persist, to control, or to limit the so-called health state of an individual in his or her particular subsystem or the suprasystem—the milieu—for a period of time. In other sections of this text, individual coping behavior, both adaptive and maladaptive, will be examined. This examination will demonstrate that individual responses to stressors are often systematically identifiable and modifiable in ways that promote health.

THE PSYCHOSOCIAL ASPECTS OF BEHAVIOR

Overview

The unique personality of each individual is a production of numerous influences, including the range of interactions and regulatory influences in his or her internal and external milieu. Each person is presumably responding to these influences and experiencing the consequences of the interactions from the time of earliest embryonic life to maturity (Kolb, 1977). The primary limitations that exist are in the potentials for individual development, that is, the inheritance component that is somewhat consistent with the species (including the individual's sex), and the quality and quantity of the supportive and restrictive elements that influence the physical and emotional maturational process. For example, restrictive elements such as intelligence, emotional and physical coordination, sensory acuity, potential for memory storage and retrieval, and general or special responsiveness of the individual to available stimuli are each governed by the nervous system and the related hormonal and humoral regulators. Of comparable importance are the quality and quantity of the supportive elements of nutrition (food essentials, vitamins, minerals, water); emotional, spiritual, and physical stimulation and development opportunities (interaction with others of the species, maneuverability and balance in the overall environment); and protection (shelter, clothing, institutional).

The complex internal and external environment, then, tests the potential of the individual continuously. Through a system of supports, challenges, crises, and interactions and the consequences of the accumulations (the feedback loop of the system), behavior patterns emerge and the development of personality occurs.

In order to increase an understanding of *personality*, it is helpful to explore it by definition as well as theory. Therefore, this section includes several definitions of personality and a discussion of several prominent theories of personality and learning in Western culture.

Theories of Personality

Historically, the study of the development of personality and the self as revealed to others has included three approaches. Maier (1965) identified these as the psychoanalytic, the exploration of learned behavior, and the investigation of cognitive functioning. Several definitions of personality and brief summaries of the theoretical bases of these three approaches are presented here in order to illustrate the significance of the psycho-social-cultural variable in the several theories.

Psychoanalytic Influences

Many early twentieth century personality theorists were largely influenced by the Freudian psychoanalytical explanations of personality development in which the trio of the id, ego, and superego comprised the three behavioral dynamics. This trio emerged from an energy or drive that existed from birth, the libido, or a psychosexual energy that generated all psychological processes (Freud, in Strachey, 1958). These were identified briefly as follows. The id comprised the sum of the excessive wishes and originated in the unconsciousness of the individual. These desires were psychologically controlled by the ego, which is responsible for synthesizing and integrating the past experiences of the individual in terms of present tasks. The ego offered almost entirely conscious direction and was influenced by the superego, or conscience, developed through the personal experiences and the directions of "significant others" in one's life. In the well-integrated personality, behavior satisfactorily met the demands of these three dynamics.

Subsequent interpersonal theories of Horney, Jung, Rank, Sullivan, and Erikson evolved from the psychoanalytic theory of personality development in which the primary emphasis was on the conscious and unconscious emotional processes as motivational forces. The social interactions, according to the theory, were components of the integrated experiences as well as controllers of the superego.

The work of Erikson extended the basic psychoanalytic theories of development through the integration of concepts from cultural anthropology, social psychology, child development, Gestaltism, literature, art, and history (Maier, 1965).

Erikson (1963) stated that the individual developed into a defined self within a social reality. The identity of the self developed from the gradual integration of all of the identifications the individual had made. For example, as the child developed, he or she identified himself or herself with habits, traits, occupations, and ideas in interactions with others or through observations of their interactions in the environment. The meaningfulness to the individual of these models depended upon their fulfillment of the appropriate maturational stage requirements and the synthesis habits of the ego. The development of the individual, according to Erikson, was dependent upon a socialization process in which the ego integrated the person's timetable with the structure of the social institutions.

Learning Theory Influences

Emphasis on the importance of learned behavior as a foundation for a study of personality was not a novel approach for the American behaviorists of the early twentieth century. It emerged (perhaps with more fervor than other concepts) from the tabula rasa view of the mind. However, the early American behaviorists—particularly Watson (1920)—sought to remove the term *personality* from the study of psychology and substitute

TABLE 2-1.

A COMPARISON OF THE MAJOR THEORETICAL CONTRIBUTIONS OF FREUD, SULLIVAN, ERIKSON, AND PIAGET

Sigmund Freud (1856-1939)	Harry Stack Sullivan (1892-1949)	Eric Erikson	Jean Paul Piaget
1) First to identify and classify developmental stages.	1) First to focus on the interactional process between mother and child.	1) First to include adulthood as a stage of growth and focus on the formation of personal identity as a key concept.	1) First to be concerned with the development of cognition.
2) Theory focused on the concept of libidinal energy and instinctual drives as the forces which motivate behavior.	2) Theory focused on the concept of anxiety as the dynamic force in the developmental process.	2) Theory combines Freud's biological or heredity factors with Sullivan's social factors.	2) The theory concentrates on the development of intellectual capabilities with little reference to emotional or social development.
3) Developed the concept that the mind operates on three levels—the unconscious, the preconscious and the conscious. Emphasis placed on intrapsychic behavior.	3) Used Freud's concept of the unconscious and conscious mind. Emphasis placed on observable behavior.	3) Used Freud's concept of the divisions of the mind. Emphasis placed on the individual's relationship as influenced by the family, peers and society.	3) Emphasized the dual process of assimilation and accommodation with respect to the development of reasoning, language, intelligence, and the concepts of nature, time, space and causality.
4) Experience is always viewed in relation to unconscious material and reconstruction of the past.	4) Experience is viewed as an interactional process existing between self and others, which depends on previous experience.	4) Experience is viewed as a dichotomy established between basic attitudinal values and feelings.	4) Experience is viewed as a building-block process for the expansion of intrinsic capabilities.
5) The mind has a structural division—the id, the ego and the superego.	5) Experience is divided into three cognitive modes—prototaxic, parataxic, and syntaxic.	5) The extended social experience is the primary framework in learning.	5) Development is influenced by individual differences and social influences; focus is on the mind rather than on the self.

TABLE 2-1 (Continued).

Sigmund Freud (1856-1939)	Harry Stack Sullivan (1892-1949)	Eric Erikson	Jean Paul Piaget
6) Developed theories while working with pathological adults, primarily neurotics.	6) Developed theories while working with pathological adults, primarily schizophrenics.	6) Developed theories while working with children and emphasized both health and illness in the personality.	6) Developed theories while working with normal, healthy children.
7) Believed that no behavioral change can be effected without understanding the content and meaning of the individual's unconscious.	7) Believed that change occurs only when improved interpersonal relationships are combined with an understanding of the basic good-bad influences.	7) Believed that behavioral change occurs only when the individual achieves integration of aptitudes, libido and social roles to form a stronger ego identity.	7) Believed that change occurs as an outcome of the socialization process.
8) Focused on emotional development.	8) Focused on emotional and interpersonal development.	8) Focused on emotional, interpersonal and spiritual development.	8) Focused on intellectual and psychomotor skill development.

Source: Helen Z. Kreigh and Joanne E. Perko, *Psychiatric and Mental Health Nursing: A Commitment to Care and Concern.*

© 1979 by Reston Publishing Company, Inc.

TABLE 2-2.
A COMPARISON OF THE DEVELOPMENT STAGES POSTULATED BY FREUD, SULLIVAN, ERIKSON, AND PIAGET

Freud	Sullivan	Erikson	Piaget
I) Oral Stage (0-18 months) a) The mouth is a source of satisfaction. b) Two Phases: 1) Passive Only interests are satisfying hunger and *sucking* Completely helpless, *security* is the greatest need. Narcissistic and egocentric, operates on *pleasure principle.* Omnipotent feelings are prevalent. 2) Active Biting is a mode of pleasure. Continuous experimentation and associations. Sensory discriminations. Differentiation be-	I) Infancy (0-18 months) a) The mouth is a source of satisfaction. b) Mouth—takes in (sucking), cuts off (biting), and pushes out (spitting) objects introduced by others. c) Crying, babbling and cooing are modes of communication used by the infant to call attention of adults to self. d) *Satisfaction response* (PLEASURE PRINCIPLE) Infant's biological needs are met and a mutual feeling of comfort and fulfillment is experienced by mother and child. (Mother gives and child takes.) e) *Empathic observation* Capacity to perceive feelings of others as his own immediate	I) Oral-sensory Stage (0-12 months) a) The mouth is a source of satisfaction and a means of dealing with anxiety producing situations. b) Focus is on the development of the *basic attitudes of trust vs. mistrust.* c) Attitudes are formed through mother's reaction to infant needs.	I) Sensorimotor Stage (0-12 months) a) Emphasis in on *pre-verbal intellecutal* development. b) Learns relationships with external objects. c) Focus is on physical development with gradual increase in ability to think and use language.

TABLE 2-2 (Continued).

Freud	Sullivan	Erikson	Piaget
	tween mental images and reality. Differentiation of others and discovery of self.		
	f) *Autistic invention* State of symbol activity in which the infant feels he is master of all he surveys.		
	g) Experimentation, exploration and manipulation are methods used to acquaint self with environment.		
II) Anal Stage (1½-3 years)	II) Childhood (1½-6 years)	II) Anal-muscular Stage (1-3 years)	II) Preoperational Stage (2-7 years)
a) Primary activity is on learning muscular control association with urination and defecation. *(toilet training period)*	a) Begins with the capacity for communicating through speech and ends with a beginning need for association with peers.	a) Learns the extent to which the *environment* can be influenced by direct manipulation.	a) Learns to use *symbols and language.*
b) Exhibits more self control; walks, talks, dresses and undresses	b) Uses *language* as a tool to communicate wishes and needs.	b) Focuses on the development of the *basic attitudes of autonomy vs shame and doubt.*	b) Learns to *imitate* and play.
c) *Negativism*—assertion of independence.	c) Anus is power tool used to give or withhold a part of self to control significant people in his environment.	c) Exerts self-control and will power.	c) Displays *egocentricity.*
d) Introduction of *reality principle, ego development.*			d) Engages in *animistic thinking*—endowment of objects with power and ability.

Freud	Sullivan	Erikson	Piaget
e) Superego begins to develop. f) Engages in *parallel play*.	d) Emergence and integration of *self-concept* and *reflected appraisal of significant persons*. e) Awareness that postponing or delaying gratification of own wishes may bring satisfaction. f) Begins to find limits in experimentation, exploration and manipulation. g) More aggressive. h) Uses parallel play and curiosity to explore environment. i) Uses exhibitionism and mastubatory activity to become acquainted with self and others. j) Demonstrates a beginning ability to think abstractly.		

TABLE 2-2 (Continued)

Freud	Sullivan	Erikson	Piaget
III) Phallic Stage (3-6 years) a) *Libidinal energy focus on the genitals.* b) Learns *sexual identity.* c) *Superego becomes internalized.* d) *Sibling rivalry and manipulation of parents occurs.* e) Intellectual and motor facilities are refined. f) Increased socialization and associative play.		III) Genital-locomotor Stage (3-6 years) a) Learns the extent to which being *assertive* will influence the environment. b) Focus is on the development of *the basic attitudes of initiative vs. guilt.* c) Explores the world with senses, thoughts and imagination. d) Activities demonstrate direction and purpose. e) Engages in first real social contacts through *cooperative play.* f) *Develops conscience.*	III) Concrete operations Stage (7-11 years) a) Deals with visible concrete objects and relationships. b) Increased intellectual and conceptual development—employs
IV) Latency (6-12 years) a) *Quiet stage in which sexual development lies dormant,* emotional tension eases. b) *Normal homosexual phase* For boys, gangs	III) Juvenile Stage (6-9 years) a) Learns to form satisfactory relationship with peers. b) *Peer norms prevail* over family norms. c) Engages in *competi-*	IV) Latency (6-12 years) a) Learns to utilize energy to create, develop and manipulate. b) Focus is on the development of *basic attitudes of industry vs. inferiority.*	

Freud	Sullivan	Erikson	Piaget
For girls, cliques ' c) Increased intellectual capacity. d) Starts school. e) Identifies with teachers and peers. f) Weakening of home ties. g) Recognizes authority figures outside home, age of hero worship.	tion, experimentation, exploration and manipulation. d) Able to cooperate and compromise. e) Demonstrates capacity to love. f) Distinguishes fantasy from reality. g) Exerts internal control over behavior. IV) Preadolescence (9-12 years) a) Learns to relate to a friend of the same sex—chum relationship. b) Concerned with group success and derives satisfaction from group accomplishment. c) Shows signs of rebellion—restlessness, hostility, irritability. d) Assumes less responsibility for own actions. e) Moves from egocentricity to a more full social state.	c) Able to initiate and complete tasks. d) Understands rules and regulations. e) Displays competence and productivity.	logic and reasoning. c) More socialized and rule conscious.

TABLE 2-2 (Continued)

Freud	Sullivan	Erikson	Piaget
	f) Uses experimentation, exploration, manipulation. g) Seeks *consensual validation* from peers.		IV) Formal Operations Stage (11-15 years) a) Develops *true abstract thought*. b) Formulates hypothesis and applies logical tests. c) *Conceptual independence*.
V) Genital Stage (12-Early Adulthood) a) Appearance of secondary sex characteristics, *reawakening of sex drives*. b) Increased concern over physical appearance. c) Strives toward *independence*. d) Development of *sexual maturity*. e) *Identity crisis*. f) Identification of love object of opposite sex. g) Intellectual Maturity. h) Plans future.	V) Early Adolescence (12-14 years) a) Experience physiological changes. b) Uses rebellion to gain Independence. c) Fantasizes, over-identifies with heroes. d) Discovers and begins relationships with opposite sex. e) Demonstrate *heightened levels of anxiety* in most interpersonal relationships.	V) Puberty and Adolescence (12-18 years) a) Demonstrates an ability to *integrate life experiences*. b) Focus is on the development of the *basic attitudes of identity vs. role diffusion*. c) Seeks partner of the opposite sex. d) Begins to establish his identity and place in society.	

Freud	Sullivan	Erikson	Piaget
	VII) Late Adolescence (14-21 years) a) Establishes an enduring intimate relationship with one member of the opposite sex. b) Self-concept becomes stabilized. c) Attains physical maturity. d) Develops ability to use logic and abstract concepts.	VI) Young Adulthood (18-25 years) a) Primarily concerned with developing an intimate relationship with another adult. b) Focus is on the development of the basic attitudes of intimacy and solidarity vs. isolation.	
	VII) Adulthood (21 years +) a) Assumes responsibility relevant to station in life. b) Maintains balance and involvement between self, family and community. c) Further develops creativity. d) Reaffirms values in life.	VII) Adulthood (25-45 years) a) Primarily concerned with establishing and maintaining a family. b) Focus is on the development of the basic attitudes of generativity vs. stagnation. c) Displays a marked degree of creativity. d) Adjust to circumstances of middle age. e) Re-evaluates life's accomplishments and goals.	

TABLE 2-2 (Continued)

Freud	Sullivan	Erikson	Piaget
		VIII) Maturity (older than 45 years) a) *Acceptance of life style as meaningful and fulfilling.* b) *Focus is on the development of basic attitudes of ego integrity vs. despair.* c) Remains optimistic and continues to grow. d) Adjusts to limitations. e) Adjusts to retirement. f) Adjusts to reorganized family patterns. g) Adjusts to losses. h) Accepts death with serenity.	

Source: Helen Z. Kreigh and Joanne E. Perko, *Psychiatric and Mental Health Nursing: A Commitment to Care and Concern.*
© **1979** by Reston Publishing Company, Inc.

the study of "objectively observed natural events" as a method for learning about the prediction of behavior and individual development. The focus was on measurable performance and the eventual use of the experimental method, which contrasted outcomes of procedures to demonstrate the importance of the contingencies within the environment as influencers of behavior.

Prominent contributors to the learned-behavior theory have included Hull, Dollard, Miller, Mowrer, Sears, Whiting, and Skinner (Maier, 1965). Sears sought to reconcile psychoanalytic and behavior theory. His concept of individual development implied that social conditions dictated the emergence of developmental phases. Development was viewed as a continuous orderly sequence of conditions that created the actions and eventual behavior patterns (Sears, Maccoby, & Levin 1957). Child development, therefore, was a consequence of learning. For Whiting and Child (1953), personality was defined as an unseen mediational process between observable input and output variables. These theorists did not deal with the mediating factors only, but also with the variables involved.

Skinner (1974) defined personality as a repertoire of behavior given by an organized set of contingencies. He stated that the genetic endowment of the individual was nothing (again, the continuation of the tabula rasa concept) until it had been acted upon by the environment, through which immediate changes were produced. His work with a variety of species studied through varied experimental and observational conditions was exceedingly influential in the development and expansion of a reinforcement theory of learning.

Cognitive Theory Influences

The primary emphasis on a cognitive theory as a foundation for the study of personality has been largely the work of Piaget, who sought a link between psychology and biology. After extensive qualitative study of human behavior over a range of developmental patterns, Piaget concluded that the attributes of personality depended upon the intellectual capacity of the individual to organize experience. In turn, these experiences influenced the interests and pursuits of the individual and those interests he or she tended to pursue (1957). Further, Piaget saw learning as a function of development rather than as an independent process or function.

Piaget observed in his studies of the experiences of children that the stages of cognition progressed from the sensori-motor level of the nursery toddler group, to pre-operational and intuitive, to concrete operations, and finally to formal operations, problem-solving and synthesis, at puberty.

Further, Selman (1977) identified four interpersonal stages of social cognitive development, almost parallel to Piaget's stages of development. The interpersonal stage progresses from the one person subjective view of the young child to a mutual perspective stage wherein reciprocal relationships are possible, to a third person view capable of empathy by middle childhood, and finally, to the broader view of perspective in which complex relationships are possible in an individual approaching adulthood.

Thus, in each of the above orientations to cognitive development, the organization of experience appeared integral in the formation of personality and interpretation of behavior.

Other definitions of personality and the theories represented, particularly the sociointeractive theories, will be acknowledged because of the interest they have generated in the socialization process, role development, and interactional behavior (Brim, 1960; Brim & Wheeler, 1966).

Allport (1961), a social psychologist, defined personality as the internal dynamic organization in the individual of those psychophysical systems that determine his or her characteristic behavior and thought. In his discussion of this sociointeractive theory, Bradburn (1963) distinguished between behavior patterns specific to particular roles (e.g., mother, son, student) that the individual performed and the role that was general in terms of all roles. He concluded that the latter constituted a definition of personality, that is, the generalized patterns of behavior characteristic of the individual under a variety of environmental conditions constituted the personality that pervaded all roles.

This construction accounted for the inconsistencies of the behavior of an individual over time as well as his or her preferences for particular types of activities.

Kolb (1977) presented a unified conceptual definition of personality in his statement that personality was the distinctive whole formed by the relatively permanent patterns of behavior and tendencies of the given individual. This development depended upon a series of social interactions that tended to be enduring and consistent relative to attitude, beliefs, desires, values, and patterns of adaptation (or coping), thereby making each individual unique.

The definitions of personality as part of the overall discussion of the psychosocial aspects of behavior influenced the development and interpretations of the theories of learning. A review of these differences in several prominent theories has been included here to provide the reader with an orientation to the more prominent theories in the study of the behavior of humankind.

The two principle learning theories are the stimulus-response (S-R) and the cognitive theories. However, other theories exist that may not fit readily into these two categories. These include theories of functionalism, psychodynamics, and the probabilistic model builders (Hilgard & Bower, 1966).

The primary differences between the S-R and cognitive learning theories have been summarized by Hilgard and Bower (1966) along the following three variables:

1. *Mediary mechanisms of learning.* The S-R theorists describe the peripheral mechanisms as the response or movement intermediaries in the integration of behavior sequences, as opposed to the central integration (ideation) of the cognitive theorists. Each view, however, depends largely upon "inference" for validity.

2. *What is learned.* The S-R theorists state that habit comprises that which is learned, whereas the cognitive theorists state that the cognitive structures are what are learned.

3. *Methods for reaching solution.* The S-R theorists state that the learner assembles his or her habits from past experiences appropriate to the new problem, seeking familiar elements or situations in the new problem. If he or she is unable to find these, the learner resorts to repeated trial and error until a solution is found. The cognitive theorists state that the learner uses insight as he or she performs perceptual structuring in order to understand and reach a solution to the problem.

A presentation of several of the primary theories from the S-R and cognitive categories follows.

The Stimulus-Response Theories and Principles

Probably the most dominant learning theory of the past half century has been the connectionism of Thorndike. He has been identified as the primary influencer of Gestaltism, conditioned-reflex theory, and sign-Gestaltism (Tolman, 1938). His theory was known as the original stimulus-response psychology of learning, in which it was theorized that an association or "bond" (connection) developed between sense impressions and action impulses. These bonds became stronger or weaker under the conditions of practice, which included readiness on the part of the learner and the consequences of the impulses to the learner. Thorndike minimized the role of understanding, emphasized the theory of transfer, viewed reward as motivation, and recognized the law of disuse (decay without practice) (Thorndike, 1932, 1933, 1949).

The Classical Conditioning Theory of Pavlov was often identified as the reflex theory in which the unconditioned stimulus and unconditioned reflex became the conditioned stimulus and the conditioned reflex through the use of pairing. Pavlov demonstrated experimental extinction with the decline of reinforcement and a precise methodology (1927). American psychologists have substituted "conditioned response" instead of conditioned reflex as they continued to study the impact of this particular experimentation and other Pavlovian works.

As interest in classical conditioning and methodology developed, several other theories of learning emerged that depended in part upon the S-R association psychology. These theories had commonalities that included the necessity to study overtly observable stimuli and measurable responses relative to the individual, that is, studies of identifiable behavior that were deemed to be outcomes of particular events. The events were largely in the form of physical stimuli observed to induce a change of behavior (a response), with the intermediary processes within the individual largely inferred.

Principles and Theories of Reinforcement

The central principles that had been recognized in the classical conditioning experiments of Pavlov, and his associates (e.g., paired association) and the connectionism of Thorndike (e.g., the law of effect), emerged as the principle of reinforcement primarily as a consequence of the work of an American psychologist, Skinner (1938). Skinner observed in his animal laboratories that learning was under the control of its consequences (1938). He identified this form of behavior as *operant,* in contrast to the more conventional stimulus-response behavior psychology, which proposed that the connection between the stimulus and response was of greater significance than that between the reward and response espoused by many of his peers. Whereas the elicited responses were obtained through the use of known stimuli in the S-R paradigm, the operant behavior was an emitted response not necessarily correlated with known stimuli. It operated on the environment to satisfy needs of the individual, thereby leading to reinforcement. Any stimulus was considered a reinforcer if it increased the probability of the response (Skinner, 1953). An example of operant conditioning may be observed in the behavior of two young boys in a two-bed hospital unit:

The older child wished to be alone in the room and banged the door loudly as he entered and left the hospital room, thereby arousing the other youth and causing him to cry for his mother or nurse because of the disturbance. On a particular occasion, the older boy released the door and it closed quietly, therefore, the other child did not awaken and cry. This response acted as stimulus or reinforcer for the continuation of the "quieter door closing" behavior of the older child and its reinforcing potential increased with each occurrence. Thus, the stimulus (child did not cry) was a reinforcer since it increased the probability of the response of quiet door closing.

An important feature of operant conditioning over the conditioning of respondent behavior of the S-R theories was identified as the condition that the stimuli for emitted behavior need not be specified, in contrast to the stimuli of S-R elicited behavior. This explained the production of the original or novel behavior observed in creative or artistic endeavors.

Ferster and Skinner (1957) published a review of their early learning research in which the nomenclature and descriptions of their experimental programs of reinforcement were included. These programs have been tested repeatedly by numbers of investigators and have added to the knowledge of learning and influenced the development and practice of behavior modification in humankind.

An important aspect of this research has been the exploration of the function of secondary reinforcement and the emergence of generalized reinforcers. Skinner (1953) explained that generalization occurred as some secondary reinforcers—stimuli that acquired reinforcing ability through association with primary (or natural) reinforcing stimuli—tended to accompany varied primary reinforcers. For example, money became a generalized reinforcer as it acquired reinforcing value for a number of activities, thereby providing access to food, shelter, and other materials.

The critics of the Skinnerian operant approaches to changes in behavior, although they agreed that the systematic approaches did modify performance, stated their opposition to the extent of the manipulation and control of the individual.

Skinner responded that the individual contingencies need not be exploitative, that those stimuli in control of another (as in teaching verbal behavior) eventually became influenced and controlled by the learner and balanced by the unarranged contingencies with equal power (plus the possibilities of unhappy consequences). Further, Skinner (1974) explained that the theoretical applications of the scientific operant methods described maximize the control exerted by the stimulus and minimize the incidental effects.

Summary of S-R Theory

The S-R respondent behavior psychology theory and the operant conditioning principles advocated by Skinner have contributed to the broad theory of reinforcement. Within the S-R theory, the principles include the importance of the active learner, that is, the learner response and learning by doing; the frequency of repetition needed for skill acquisition; the use of reinforcement and attentiveness to schedules; the generalization and discrimination effects as extenders and expanders of the learning matter; the introduction of models and attentiveness to cues in order to enhance novelty in behavior; and the need to deal with drives and motivations (Hilgard & Bower, 1966).

Within the operant approach, in which shaping through reinforcement modifies behavior, the major principles include the requisite for immediate reinforcement; attention to the emitted behavior; the need for a gradual progression from simple to more complex behaviors (shaping); the effects of the gradual withdrawal of stimulus support (fading of the response); the importance of attentiveness as a method of learning; and the development of abstract and conceptual abilities through discrimination training (Holland, 1960).

The Unified Theory of Gagné

Gagné developed a hierarchical model as a unified theory of conditioned learning in which eight categories of simple to complex learning were dependent upon the mastery of each preceding category (Gagné, 1965). The categories included signal learning (similar to classical conditioning); S-R learning; chaining (the acquired behavior as a chain of two or more S-R connections); verbal associations (learning of verbal chains); multiple discrimination (different responses to many different stimuli that resemble each other); concept learning (response to a class of stimuli); principle learning (a chain of stimuli or concepts); and problem solving (the use of a combination of principles to produce a higher order capability) (Gagné, 1965). A major contribution of this theory was the emphasis on the structure of knowledge, also expressed by Bruner (1964) and Piaget (1952) in their discussions of abstract and concrete knowledge.

Cognitive Theory

The Cognitive Learning Theory (Gilbert, 1962) emphasized concepts of the organization of meaningful wholes (simple wholes to complex wholes, not "parts to wholes"); perceptual features that show interrelatedness (x leads to y); learning with understanding (the necessity of meaningfulness); importance of the feedback loop in order for consequences to be acknowledged and errors to be corrected; importance of goal-setting as a determiner of behavior; and divergent and convergent thinking, which leads to an array of options for solutions to problems and to the ones that are logically correct. Gilbert postulated that numerous categories of learning exist for the individual, thereby explaining the almost infinite range of behavior that emerges through the mediational processes of the nervous system.

Psychoanalytic Theory

The Psychoanalytic Theory of Learning, influenced by Freudian and neo-Freudian theorists, emphasized the importance of the past experiences of the learner. In this developmental psychology, the principle of the capacity of the learner was primary.

Impressions of early childhood were origins for conflict, including toilet training, food, sex, and aggressive behavior. The younger the individual, the greater the capacity to learn because, given appropriate neurological maturity, he or she was more impressionable. Moreover, since particular stages in life were considered to be more conflictual than other stages, conflict-free learning should proceed during the latency period. Other principles included learning through practice as a method for "working through" conflict in order to find new angles and cues in the conflict resolution; motivation, especially the "learned drive" of anxiety and the consequences of ego threats that lead to the defense mechanisms of regression, aggression, and repression; understanding, in order for the individual to achieve cognitive control in the management of his or her conduct; transfer as a concept explaining the substitution role that was given on occasion by the client to the change agent (e.g., therapist or teacher) in the relationship; and forgetting as a primary result of the repressions that occurred early in life and were part of the accumulative storehouse in the unconscious.

Critics have acknowledged that psychoanalytic learning theory made the demarcation between normal and neurotic behavior less distinct; that is, a continuum of behavior existed instead of the so-called normal and abnormal categories (Hilgard & Bower, 1966).

The influential learning theories discussed here reveal a diversity as well as similarity in content. Each theory has been tested through applications in learning situations. However, change agents have combined theories and/or used parts of them in eclectic fashion in order to influence the learning processes of individuals, and the diversity of application has confounded the behavioral outcomes somewhat for comparative study purposes. A truly unified theory has not emerged, but a review of the major theories has confirmed that the theories often seemed to be sequential to or developed as reactions to other theories. That is, one theory was presented, examined, and its primary principles practiced as though it were "moving ahead" on previously presented theories. Or, on occasion, another theory or principle emerged that purportedly answered previously "unanswered" questions. The development of the principle of operant conditioning was an example of the latter.

Other theories of learning have been proposed more recently, including the *observational theory* (Bandura, 1962, 1965), in which principles of vicarious conditioning and extinction modify behavior. In this theory, the individual observer acquired new or novel behavior without threat to himself or herself through the observation of models interacting in particular situations. The model was able to demonstrate that the performance was within a range of possible responses (from intricate acts to emotional behavior) without undue consequences to the performer or to the observer. The reinforcement awarded the model tended to act as a powerful reinforcer for the observer, that is, observers were more likely to incorporate the modeled behavior that was rewarded or positively acknowledged in some fashion. Also, reinforcement influenced vigilance behavior in individuals, which further enhanced modeling effectiveness. Bandura and Walters (1963) summarized the three possible effects of exposure to a model for imitative purposes as follows:

1. A modeling effect, involving the transmission of precisely imitative response patterns not previously present in the observer's repertory.

2. An inhibitory or disinhibitory effect, reflected in an increase or decrease in the frequency, latency, or intensity of previously acquired observer responses that are more or less similar to those exhibited by the model.

3. A possible eliciting effect, in which the observation of a model's response serves as a cue for "releasing" similar observer responses that are neither entirely novel nor inhibited as a result of prior learning.

As a consequence of testing the use of vicarious conditioning, it was found that this particular theory application was practical and beneficial in the elimination of learned maladaptive responses and increased the opportunities for the development of prosocial behavior (Bandura, 1961; 1963; 1964).

Counterconditioning: Desensitization

The use of reciprocal inhibition (desensitization) as a form of behavior modification has been advocated by Wolpe (1948; 1952; 1958) and tested extensively in the management of fear or anxiety by him and his colleagues. The elimination of fear, anxiety, and subsequent avoidance behavior of individuals extended their range of social interaction. The theoretical base and mode of treatment used processes of conditioned inhibition through reciprocal inhibition in order to break down the maladaptive behavior in bit-by-bit fashion. The schema of Wolpe was based on the principle that sympathetic and parasympathetic responsiveness tended to be physiologically antagonistic. The basic theory incorporated muscular relaxation (Jacobson, 1938) in combination with certain other pleasurable stimulations to elicit parasympathetic responses and inhibit the dominant sympathetic anxiety responses. Some critics, however, questioned the peripheral theory of anxiety as basic to this mode of change. That is, autonomic and avoidance responses were not essentially causally linked but were coeffects that operated subcortically, as in the RAS, instead of in the autonomic nervous system. Therefore, central mediators through classical conditioning procedures produced the change.

The advocates of Wolpe's theory responded that through competing responses of sufficient strength, the counterconditioning of classical conditioning replaced original responses (Bandura, 1969). Through management in a systematic manner (bit-by-bit), greater control of the outcomes of desensitization in the three identified operational procedures occurred. These procedures included training for the individual client and the systematic application of a program in which relaxation inhibits the anxiety-provoking stimuli from selected hierarchies (Wolpe & Lazarus, 1966). Modifications of the procedures have stimulated the examination and application of this theory. The

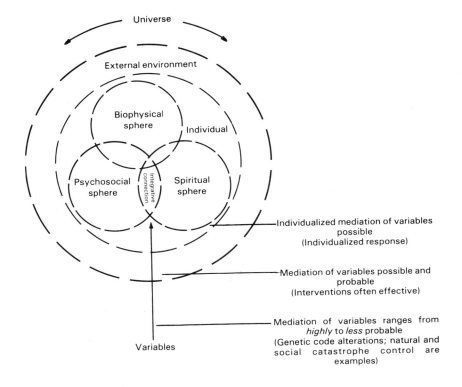

1. Mental-emotional function
2. Physical function including sensory-motor ability
3. Sociocultural experience
4. Spiritual/belief system
5. Interactive-integrative ability

In Figure 2-9, the primary spheres in the life of an individual in a complex environment, representation of the variables influencing the development of coping behavior, and probable areas for mediation are presented to depict the interactional potential among influences of human development and behavior.

FIGURE 2-9. Primary variables influencing development of human coping behavior in integrative sphere.

modifications have included the absence of the relaxation component; the use of the *in vivo* situation in contrast to the mental imagery and therapist-evoked procedures; and the advocacy of implosion (Stampfl & Levis, 1967), in which desensitization occurs through the elicitation of intense emotional responses without the occurrence of physically injurious consequences.

Whereas the theories presented here have made an impact on the designs and modalities used for health care, the deliverers of care should bear in mind that standing theories have been tested and supported, not proved. Much of the important testing for each theory has been in the application of its principles in health care settings as care providers sought to modify states of dysfunction. The interventions presented in Chapter 4 are examples of ways that care providers and their clients may be able to make further applications of the theories in enabling clients to cope effectively.

Chapter 3

How to Recognize Healthy and Unhealthy Coping Behaviors

In this chapter the concepts, definitions, and theories introduced in the two previous chapters will be applied to case studies. Case studies from the literature are included, in addition to previously unpublished examples. The purpose of examining these cases is to provide some practice in the identification of coping mechanisms that individuals, families, or groups might be using. In addition, the case studies provide opportunities to use some suggested guidelines for deciding when coping behaviors are healthy and when they are unhealthy. Chapter 4 presents some guidelines for interventions for clients displaying various aspects of coping behaviors, and Chapter 5 discusses the implications for consultation, education, and research.

ORDERS OF COPING

It is important to consider first the interpersonal relationship orders involved in coping behaviors (Figure 3-1). The first order and the simplest to conceptualize is the individual's attempt to deal with a situation that is threatening. In the health care setting at least three categories of people must cope: clients, family members, and health care providers. Each has at least three threatening agents for which coping strategies must be developed. The client must cope with illness, family, and health care personnel. The client's family must deal with the threat to its goals as imposed by the client's illness; each family member must cope with other family members; and they all must cope with the frustrations imposed upon them by the health care providers. Health care providers must cope with their reactions to clients and their illnesses; they must also cope with the client's family, as well as with other providers. Further, providers must cope with more than one client simultaneously as they attempt to provide each one with the unique caring required.

The second order of coping relationships refers to helping others cope. Again, in the health care situation there are three categories of individuals who may or may not be concerned with helping others to cope. The client often does not have only self to consider; there are also spouse and/or other relatives and

Order I: Individual encountering situations that are threatening.
Includes:

1. Client encountering current threats to health.
   Client encountering overt or covert demands from family members.
   Client encountering health care providers who may be threatening to identity, independence, job, and relationships.

2. Family members encountering client who may be "using the illness to make demands" (either realistic or unrealistic).
   Family member encountering other family members who may expect one of its members to "do something," as a child expecting mother to make daddy well.
   Family members encountering health care providers who may expect family members to provide support that is difficult personally, financially, or in some other way.

3. Health care providers encountering client who may have expectations or demands that are threatening to the provider.
   Health care providers encountering family members with expectations and needs.
   Health care providers encountering other health care providers who are threatening because of their demands and because they do not meet the expectations of the provider.

Order II: Individual trying to help another individual cope.
Includes:

1. Client helping family members cope.
   Client helping health provider cope.*

FIGURE 3-1. Relationships involved in coping in health care settings.

2. Family member helping client cope.
   Family member helping other family members cope.
   Family member helping health care providers cope.*

3. Health care providers helping clients cope.
   Health care providers helping family members cope.
   Health care providers helping other health care providers cope.

Order III: Individual helping another individual in assisting a third individual in coping.
Includes:

1. Health care provider assisting client who is trying to help family members cope.
   Health care provider helping family member help client cope.

2. Client helping health care provider help family member cope.

3. Family member helping health care provider help client cope.

*These situations should not happen but they do. It is the responsibility of the health care provider to ensure that these situations occur only when it is clear that the client or family member can cope best if helping someone else cope.

FIGURE 3-1 *(continued)*.

friends whom the client may help to cope with the illness. Although clients should not have the added burden of helping the health care providers to cope, this may happen more frequently than anyone cares to admit.

The family is usually in a position to help the client to cope, and may indeed be strengthened by helping the providers to cope. Surely, providers should not expect this service, but to accept it graciously may meet a need of a family member to express gratitude. The health care providers do have the responsibility of strengthening the coping behaviors of the client, the family members, and other providers.

The third order of coping involves an individual helping another individual who is trying to strengthen a third person's coping attempts. As a health care provider, for example, it is necessary for you to consider ways to cope with the demands of the position, including how to react to the various patient situations encountered and how to react to family and team members as they try to help clients cope. Are family members seen as necessary evils to be avoided if possible? Do staff seem irritated with mothers of sick children? Do you appreciate the concerns of the wife of the man at the peak of his career who has just suffered a myocardial infarction? What do these persons do to you? How do they make you feel and think, and how do you deal with those feelings and thoughts? Likewise, what coping behaviors do you use for yourself in working with other health care providers? Are you overly compliant in order to avoid conflicts at any price? Do you find yourself in frequent difficulties with other providers? If so, are you overly aggressive in order to preserve your own identity? How do you cope with other health care providers? There is a growing body of literature on "burn out" that relates to ways health care providers can learn more effective means of coping (Freudenberger & Richelson, 1980; Pines, Aronson, & Kafry, 1980).

CLINICAL SITUATION EXEMPLIFYING THE NEEDS FOR COPING

To exemplify the three orders of coping, the birth of an unhealthy baby will be used. The description that follows will illustrate the coping behaviors of the mother, her family, and the health care providers in that clinical setting.

The birth of a baby is recognized as a crisis for all involved, as it represents a situation of impending change. Having a baby is usually considered to be a normal developmental crisis in which the mother, father, and grandparents are supposed to be proud of the baby and quite pleased with themselves. Even the most ideal situation requires coping with changes that a baby makes in any family's arrangements. However, the birth of a baby with a congenital defect is a significant and extremely unhappy crisis.

In many cultures the mother is the primary figure who has to cope, and she shares this task with other members of her family. Within the first order of coping, the mother has to deal with her own reactions in sorting out what having a child with a defect means to her. Her thoughts and subsequent behaviors will be influenced by whether she wanted this child or resented the pregnancy. Guilt could be a factor with which she must cope if she believes that something she did caused the baby's deformity. She may be consumed with anger if she had wanted to have an abortion, but her husband or her physician talked her out of it. On the other hand, if she really wanted this baby, grief, disappointment, and sense of failure may be the feelings with which she must cope. Whether the mother has other children at all and, if so, whether the children are the same or the opposite sex of this child will influence her feelings. Consider, for example, the mother of a new baby boy who is married to a man who has three daughters from a previous marriage and who very much wanted a son. This mother will have different feelings from the mother who already has four sons. Also, the mother who has one or more other children with congenital deformities will have a different set of feelings from the mother who has three older normal children.

The mother's religious orientation or philosophy will influence how she copes; she may believe this baby is punishment for her sins. She may believe that all life is sacred and must be preserved at all costs regardless of what the financial and emotional burdens might be. On the other hand, her response may be to deny responsibility for the infant and to refuse to cooperate in the initiation of life-saving measures for the baby. Of course, the degree of the deformity and the possibility of the correction of the defect will be the influencing factors.

In the second order of coping relationships, the interaction of the mother and the baby's father influences maternal coping. The stress of sharing the parenthood of a defective child could be a bond that strengthens their marital relationship by their mutual support and understanding, including working together to solve problems and make decisions. In contrast, such an event could precipitate each partner's "blaming" the other for this tragedy and serve as a wedge that drives the family apart. Also in the second coping relationship order, the mother has to deal with her parents. If the mother is an only child, the favorite child, or the only daughter, the sense of having failed her parents may be greater than if she is one of several daughters. The mother's dependence on her parents and her success at establishing her own identity are important variables. Some mothers report receiving considerable needed support and comfort from their parents; others feel hurt that their parents viewed the event as a great tragedy and tended to be rather melodramatic.

The third relationship order of coping involves the mother's coping with her husband's responses to his parents and her parents. Again, threatening situations can serve to sever relationships that were already shaky, or they can cement and strengthen what were previously lukewarm family ties. The mother may also have to smooth the way for her other children to cope with the birth of their deformed sibling. They need to be encouraged to share their feelings with each other and their parents; they also need information as it becomes available on what to expect from their young sibling and why mother has to be away from home so much with the new baby or why the new baby died. The mother's relationship with her own siblings and how they respond to the birth of a deformed niece or nephew may become an issue. If the mother's siblings are older than she, there is the problem of sibling rivalry and whose children get the most attention from their grandparents or whose children are smarter or prettier.

The father also has to cope, and his responses may parallel those enumerated for the mother. In addition, he may have to cope with failure for the first time in his life, as he goes to the office and, according to tradition, is supposed to pass out cigars, but really does not feel like it. What should he tell people? How does a professional athlete relate to a son who has club feet or to a daughter who has a hairlip? The other family members will have their own coping to do independent of their interactions with the mother of the baby, for grandparents, aunts, uncles, siblings, and family friends, too, had their expectations for this baby.

How do you, as a health care provider, cope with the birth of an unhealthy child? After all, birth is supposed to be a normal process with babies entering the world all rosy and crying lustily. Of course that is an exaggeration, but most health care providers expect labor, delivery, and postpartum to be somewhat routine even though personalized. How do you react to the sight of a badly disfigured baby? What are your feelings about resuscitating an infant with a severe defect? How do you cope? You may avoid the situation as much as possible, assign someone else to handle this case. You may act "professional," denying your feelings and concerns. Whatever you do, if you are in contact with the mother or family members, you are a potential role model and your coping behavior may serve as either a very effective or a very ineffective example of coping.

You, as a health care provider, also have some responsibility to assess the coping behaviors of the other health care providers. If someone who is in a key position is handling the situation badly, this reflects on the entire health care team and may affect how the patient and her family cope. For example, the nurses assigned to care for the mother's postpartal needs may increase her feelings of worthlessness, loneliness, and isolation. Likewise, if the attending physician is abrupt or gives the mother more information than she can assimilate at once, the mother may be confused, leading to feelings of stupidity and lower self-esteem. Although you may not be able to change the behaviors of the other health care providers, you can be aware of any potentially destructive behaviors and attempt to buffer those behaviors, if not prevent them.

A COMPARISON OF ADAPTIVE AND MALADAPTIVE COPING

Dunbar stated in 1945 (as quoted in Coleman, 1973) that it is often "more important to know what kind of patient has the disease than what kind of disease the patient has." Although medical science has advanced remarkably since that time, later remarks reflect the same implication:

> Indeed, most of the nation's health problems—including automobile accidents, all forms of drug addiction, alcoholism, venereal disease, obesity, many cancers, most heart disease, and most infant mortality—are primarily attributable not to shortcomings on the part of the providers but to the living conditions, ignorance, or irresponsibility of the patient. (Somers, 1972)

The implication is that many, if indeed not most, illness reflects inadequate or inappropriate coping efforts. Therefore, if poor coping caused (or contributed to) illness in the first place, it is unlikely that a person is going to choose healthy, adaptive coping behaviors for dealing with the illness. Most patients need some assistance in coping with the situation in which they find themselves, and if such help is not forthcoming, the probability is high that the situation will become worse. As Selye (1956) stated, when the stress response fails to cope adequately with a potentially disease-producing situation, the body develops "diseases of adaptation" (p. 124).

In Chapter 1, coping was defined as the process by which an individual attempts to alleviate, attenuate, or remove a stressor or a threat. In general, behaviors that accomplish the goal of relieving the organism from the stress of the threat were considered to be healthy, adaptive, effective, adequate, or appropriate. Behaviors that fall short of the goal or "cost" too much were said to be unhealthy, maladaptive, ineffective, inadequate, or inappropriate. McGrath (1970) pointed out how difficult it sometimes is to distinguish between the two ends of the continuum. McGrath used outcomes as the bases for his evaluations and indicated that ineffective coping behaviors were those that simply did not accomplish the removal of the stressor or its consequences; those that worked in the short run but were not effective if evaluated over a long period of time; and those that worked but at a high price, such as damage to the organism or his aims. One of the difficulties in evaluating effectiveness was that value judgments were involved.

Coleman (1973) stated that the outcome of coping behaviors could be evaluated in terms of adaptive and maladaptive behaviors including physiological as well as psychological responses. Coleman agreed with McGrath that attempts to define coping behaviors as adaptive or maladaptive frequently have led to controversy, but Coleman went on to say that adaptive behaviors were those that contribute to the well-being of the individual and ultimately of society while maladaptive behavior was detrimental to the individual or society (p. 173).

Millon (1969) described the development of healthy and unhealthy coping behaviors. According to Millon, healthy coping behaviors begin in the healthy child who displays flexibility in his strategies, using only those behaviors that are appropriate to the experience. When feasible, direct or task-oriented solutions will be attempted. After making a conscious and objective appraisal of the conditions of reality, the individual will initiate a sequence of behaviors that have previously been successful in similar situations. The individual may alter destructive elements in behavior, remove or circumvent obstacles in the way, or compromise goals and accept substitutes. If all previously learned behaviors fail, the individual may devise some new and innovative ones. The new ones will be tested, and if adequate to the task, they will be used again in a similar situation. If the new behaviors are inadequate, the individual will try others, and so on until an adequate solution is found.

Included along with the rational and conscious task-oriented behaviors are the intrapsychic or unconscious mental processes. These unconscious mechanisms serve to ameliorate the pain and discomfort the individual is experiencing until he or she can come up with a better solution. They also help the individual to maintain his or her equilibrium until the problem can be approached more directly. Millon noted that healthy coping may be characterized by retreat and self-deception if the objective conditions of the environment prevent a direct solution to a painful problem. "It is not unrealistic and maladaptive to back off and soothe one's wounds if one cannot succeed. Only when the individual persistently distorts and denies the events of the objective world do these unconscious mechanisms interfere with effective functioning" (Millon, 1969, p. 191).

Whereas conscious coping mechanisms are not always healthy ("I need a drink" or "It's hopeless, I'll kill myself"), unhealthy coping behaviors develop as the individual becomes more and more dependent on the unconscious mechanisms and less and less active in his or her attempts to solve the problems directly. The repeated use of unconscious coping behaviors until they become habits becomes what is generally known as psychopathology. Millon (1969) identified eight coping strategies that underlie the overt manifestations of psychopathology. These strategies frequently prove to be self-defeating because they foster rather than resolve conflicts.

A review of a series of client case illustrations will provide examples of these coping strategies. The illustrations show how these individuals integrated particular maladaptive behavior into their personalities. In addition, the clients depicted in the illustrations provide opportunities to contrast the ranges of individual demographic characteristics showing that age, sex, or socioeconomic variables are only relatively influential in the development of these behaviors.

Examples of the Eight Coping Strategies

Passive-Detached

> *The passive-detached strategy* is characterized by social impassivity; affectionate needs and emotional needs are minimal, and the individual functions as a passive observer detached from the rewards and affections, as well as from the dangers of human relationships. (Millon, 1969, p. 92)

VELDA

Velda came to the school as a 12-year-old seventh grade student with neither exuberance nor overt reluctance. She had to arrive at least one-half hour before her classmates because her sister (with whom she made her home) had to "drop her off" before driving on to her own secretarial job. This enabled Velda to survey that part of the school area occupied by seventh graders until the first bell called the students to class, and stake out her particular territory. She must have known that her timing enabled her to have any spot she desired, including choices of swings, gymnasium chains, benches, or positions on the steps. However, Velda always was observed by the teachers or other students to be against the wall of the building. She rarely changed her site or body position. She seemed aloof as she watched the active schoolyard scene each morning, but she never moved far from the other students. She seemed to know everything that happened, and when questioned she could tell her sister the details of the play, clothing worn, and general gaiety or mischief on the schoolyard. She appeared to accept the role of passive observer because she never attempted to join another individual or group. However, she spoke when greeted and filed into the building in an orderly manner at the sound of the bell. Her classroom responses usually indicated that she had prepared her assignments, and her conduct was quite formal. She seldom passed notes or engaged in "fits of giggles" with her peers. The teachers noted on her progress reports that she was "mannerly, conscientious, and completed her assignments."

On the last day of school that year, as she walked out of the building with her classmates, a girl nearby fell back in the outgoing line and cried, "Oh, no!" On the walk was a dead bird. Immediately, several students crowded around the spot to have a better view. Velda ran back into the hall, where the school nurse found her sobbing. Her parents had been victims of an automobile accident one and a half years earlier, she was finally able to utter. However, she would not permit the nurse to give her a comforting embrace; she moved closer to the wall and cried softly until she was able to control herself. Suddenly, she thanked the nurse and informed her that her sister would be waiting at the bus stop, then quickly and with composure left the building.

Later next year when Velda was absent from school because of a respiratory infection, the school nurse visited her in a local hospital. Velda expressed a reserved kind of pleasure at the visit, extending her hand toward the nurse and motioning her to a nearby chair. Velda responded to the concerns about her health mentioned by the nurse with such statements as, "They made me well"; "They will let me go home tomorrow"; "People were friendly here"; and "My sister worried a lot the night I could not breathe." When the school nurse composed her summary to post on Velda's record, she asked herself, "Emotionally, where was Velda in this event?"

Active-Detached

The active-detached strategy represents an intense mistrust of others. The individual maintains a constant vigil lest his impulses and longing for affection result in a repetition of the pain and anguish he has experienced previously; distance must be kept between himself and others. (Millon, 1969, p. 92).

MARTY

Marty, a 23-year-old graduate student, came into the student health clinic because he had a "cold and sore throat." He told the examining nurse that he needed "cold medication," but denied that he needed a detailed chest examination. He finally stated that it might be helpful, and throughout the history and examination he noted, or questioned the need for, each detail of the performance. When the nurse completed the upper respiratory and chest assessment, she informed him that the physician would need to check him again because of the presence of particular chest sounds. She was aware of his watchfulness; therefore, she reiterated that the physician's check was merely a necessary confirmation, nothing for alarm but that she sensed concern about his thoughts of a possible hospitalization. He seemed to draw away physically and emotionally as he turned from the nurse and asked in a matter-of-fact manner whether or not the physician were a regular member of the staff.

On admission and throughout his early hospitalization, he questioned every request made of him and each aspect of his treatment. He confided to the nursing assistant on the third day that he must be wary of the young female nurses, interns, and physician-assistants because some of them would consider him to be a "good catch," hence his need to maintain a distance at all times. Later that evening, his temperature became sharply elevated, a chest pain appeared, and his apprehension was overtly manifested. His physician diagnosed his problem as pneumonia and ordered that he be moved to the medical intensive care unit. When he reviewed the patient's record, he noted that no entry was made in the "person to be notified in an emergency" blank and that he was of single status. He asked

Marty if he wished to call someone: a friend or relative. Marty mumbled, "No, she left for good. Can't trust a female, can you? All of them will leave sooner or later."

Marty spent the subsequent 24 hours in the intensive care unit, watching the actions of the personnel and the equipment every waking moment. During this period, he said that he was fearful that he would be forgotten when left alone; that his knowledge of electronics made him question the seemingly complete reliance by personnel on monitoring equipment; and that he was suspicious of hospital personnel who used "psych" techniques to encourage him to talk. Although he made an uneventful recovery after this critical episode, he continued to maintain the self-imposed gulf between himself and others. Eventually, he resorted to caustic responses and bitter humor when female caretakers were present. His physical recovery was uneventful and after ten days he was dismissed to his own apartment and self-care.

Passive-Dependent

The passive-dependent strategy is characterized by a search for relationships in which one can lean upon others for affection, security, and leadership (Millon, 1969, p. 92). This individual lacks both initiative and autonomy. "He has learned to assume a passive role in interpersonal relations, accepting whatever kindness and support he may find, and willingly submitting to the wishes of others in order to maintain their affection" (Millon, 1969, p. 92).

MELODY

Melody was a physically attractive, rather shy 15-year-old high school student who was assigned to a temporary shelter while awaiting placement in a fifth foster home. The social worker was unable to identify any particular rationale for her frequent home placements, but did acknowledge that the mother figure in the last home reported that Melody and the husband of the foster mother were "too cozy" in their relationship. Melody's behavior was characterized by attempts to please others as she performed the helper role; that is, she often smiled at others while moving closer physically if that seemed indicated, nodding, agreeing, or saying that she was happy to have such a person for a friend. Often it appeared to an observer that she never examined the motives or requests of others, but merely fulfilled their wishes in order to be with and accepted by them, regardless of their sex. She rarely initiated an action or expressed her own personal thoughts to others. Noticeably absent from her conversations was the opener, "I think . . ."

An examination of her case history revealed that her mother was admitted to a psychiatric hospital for care following a severely depressed state (postpartal psychosis) with the birth of Melody's younger brother. Subsequently, Melody and her brother lived with their maternal grandparents until the grandmother's death when Melody and her brother were five and three years of age, respectively. After the grandmother's death a series of foster care services were instigated, which separated the children while the absent father equivocated about placement procedures. At 15 years of age, Melody was not considered "adoptable" by the social worker.

During a very active basketball practice in a neighborhood gymnasium one afternoon, Melody suddenly placed her hands over the right lower quadrant of her abdomen and bent her body toward her knee. Her friends on the court were fearful that she had been injured in the game, but it was quickly found that she was experiencing another kind of severe pain.

After the crisis, which included emergency care and an appendectomy, Melody appeared to respond well to the physical treatment. However, she was reluctant to assume even moderate levels of self-care. She appeared exceedingly appreciative of the personal care administered by others and expressed her gratitude with apparent sincerity and poignancy. This response to the caregivers unwittingly tended to reinforce Melody's dependency behavior. She did not have to perform for herself, but languished in the security of the nurses and other caregivers. Inadvertently, it seemed, while overresponding to the wishes of the individuals in the environment, giving the caregivers feedback for their attention, Melody was continuing the sick-role behavior beyond its ordinary protective boundaries. In return, she had the attention and supposedly the affection of the individuals whose initial goals included returning Melody to a state of physical and emotional independence following a crisis. Unfortunately, Melody was classified as a good patient because of her pleasant acceptance of the ministrations of the hospital staff, but the assessment of a skillful nurse-consultant noted that the goals of recovery for Melody were unmet.

Melody had valued affection and kindness in ways that fostered dependence, misdirected the early interventive strategies, and prolonged her hospitalization. In fact, the consultant noted, the caregivers had overlooked their opportunity to increase Melody's initiative and autonomy during a time when, according to crisis theory concepts, their client was vulnerable to change.

Active-Dependent

In the *active-dependent strategy*, we observe an insatiable and indiscriminate search for stimulation and affection. The patient's gregarious and capricious behavior gives the appearance of considerable independence of others, but beneath this guise lies a fear of autonomy and an intense need for signs of social approval and affection. Affection must be replenished constantly and must be obtained from every source of interpersonal experience. (Millon, 1969, p. 92)

MRS. LAMAR

Mrs. Lamar was a handsome 68-year-old widow who carried herself well. She had been a resident of a privately sponsored retirement setting for less than a year, appearing to have made a reasonable adjustment to the move from her duplex apartment in a comfortable middle class neighborhood. Her only son lived in the Far East; and the decision had been made that it was not safe for her to live alone. She had delighted in decorating her efficiency apartment in the retirement residence and in presenting selected items of value to the reception rooms of the residential building. However, she soon appeared to "bustle about" as she encountered other residents and staff, always in quest of a task to perform or a favor to bestow. She was envied by many other women in the setting because of her apparent independence. The staff often commented to her and to each other (in her hearing range) that she was a model resident.

However, her assigned advisor had observed recently that she wept occasionally in the privacy of her apartment. The advisor had made several informal "pop" visits, noting that Mrs. Lamar had difficulty in "pulling herself together." She became more conspicuous in the manner in which she sought approval from others. For example, she adjusted her gift objects in the reception room with increasing frequency—always asking for the opinions of staff and residents regarding the appropriateness of placement. She seemed to be acting independently, but the slightest reluctance of an approval response from others increased her body movements (hands fluttering, head nodding, lip quivering) and decreased her smiling, verbal behavior, and appearance of satisfaction and ease with the situation. She seemed to over-respond to the hesitancy of others to offer approval and even appeared to accept it as personal rejection. Occasionally, she sought to recoup this loss of approval with actual gift-giving in the form of small objects or candies. She would appear to think of the gifts suddenly, returning to and from her quarters with "just the thing to give us a lift." The jovial acceptance of these gestures seemed to alleviate her tension, and her delight with the situation was noticeable.

During a periodic summary conference with Mrs. Lamar, the advisor was able to discover some of the rationale for her almost insatiable need for approval and affection. Mrs. Lamar had talked about the changes in the nearby residents, recounting the situations that had caused several acquaintances to be moved to settings that provided more direct care. She often lamented, "How sad it is to be removed from people you love." She had concluded this shared confidence with the comment that she was too independent to be dependent on others.

When it became necessary, because of neuromuscular degeneration, for Mrs. Lamar to relocate to a setting wherein she could obtain assistance with ambulation, she appeared to cope with the change by assuming an almost totally dependent behavior. She continued to express gratitude and affectionate statements to the individuals around her, but she decreased her self-care to a minimum level. Ultimately, the caregivers accepted this response from Mrs. Lamar, but they endeavored to maintain daily a minimal self-care level.

Passive-Independent

The *passive-independent strategy* is noted by narcissism and self-involvement. As a function of early experience, the individual has learned to overvalue his self-worth; however, his confidence in his superiority may be based on false premises. Nevertheless, he assumes that others will recognize his worth, and he maintains a self-assured distance from those whom he views to be inferior to himself. (Millon, 1969, p. 92)

MR. CHARLIE

Mr. C., as he was known to his close acquaintances at work, a 42-year-old night maintenance man in a small manufacturing plant, was the father of three sons, 11, 14, and 16 years of age. His wife, aged 40, was employed as a part-time clerk in the same business. They were regarded as a hardworking, industrious family in their south Georgia community. However, very few people in the community knew the family well because of Mr. C's aloofness and the schedule he had to keep. He often reminded his children, wife, and neighbors that they would be moving from the neighborhood very soon because he was in line for a promotion. Therefore, he was not interested in the assumption of any community responsibilities, or even in improving the value of his modest home. He gave the overall impression that the position he had held for five years—worthwhile work, but of moderate status and economic value—was temporary and that he was destined to become a foreman in the near future. Actually, his education and background were inadequate for a supervisory job, according to his record, and he had not participated in any known recent preparatory experiences. However, he seemed to value his own hard work and to believe that his supervisors would recognize this with a promotion in the near future. In his personal behavior, Mr. C. chose to "dress and travel" as a person in a higher income bracket. He was permitted to enter the plant each evening in a uniform provided by his company, but chose to wear his street suit and change after his arrival. In fact, the other workers often referred to him as the "assistant night foreman," a title he did not refute or correct because he never shared the companionship of personnel he deemed beneath his level.

Mr. C. slipped on a rain-swept ramp of a plant building one evening and fell to a semihard surface at ground level. Amazingly, he appeared not to have obtained serious injuries but was hospitalized in order to complete an evaluation and provide opportunities for medical observations.

Following emergency admission procedures and his placement in a semiprivate room in a small community hospital, Mr. C. requested that his wife obtain his suit of clothing from his locker at the plant, take his uniform home, and limit the information given to their neighbors about his condition and the events of the accident. Although his employers assumed financial responsibility for the accident-caused hospitalization, Mr. C. often appeared to expect extraordinary attention from the staff. He made numerous requests for services from the ancillary workers while remaining aloof from them, but seemed to show a particular deference to physicians and head nurses. At the time of his dismissal three days after admission, one of the nurses remarked to a peer, "I think that Mr. C. really hates to leave this place! He must have felt very comfortable here."

Active-Independent

> The *active-independent strategy* reflects a mistrust of others and a desire to assert one's autonomy; the result is an indiscriminate striving for power. Rejection of others is justified because they cannot be trusted; autonomy and initiative are claimed to be the only means of heading off betrayal by others. (Millon, 1969, p. 92)

MIKE

Mike was destined to rise over others, it seemed. Although physically unattractive because of his apparent body tension, rapid fire speech, and other mannerisms that implied impatience, he was usually able to perform any task on his engineering team with the skill and efficiency of someone older and more experienced than he was at 30 years of age. He was well-educated and had acquired the ability to attend to the cues in the environment in the most productive manner. This enabled him to solve problems effectively and to achieve status with management rapidly. A few observations of his strategies indicated that he often chose to perform in his own fashion the tasks delegated to his group. In other words, the decisions, many actions, and the development of elaborate reports were his responsibility by his own choice. When complimented for the early or highly successful completion of an assignment, he frequently stated, "If you want the best job, the best rule is to do it yourself: my motto." He often rationalized this behavior with the explanation that if one had been "let down" by peers it was difficult to trust people again, because so few were willing to do their best on difficult assignments. He appeared proud of his self-control and the knowledge that he would never let himself down.

In the midst of a physical examination required to increase his insurance coverage, Mike was diagnosed as a mild diabetic. He was able to complete the essential tests, participate in the initial educational program, and begin his regimen without hospitalization. His physician and the nurse-educator responsible for much of the educational process expressed compliments and amazement at how readily Mike demonstrated his ability for self-care. However, as Mike began to appear overly confident in his ability to manage himself with this new problem, the nurse and physician feared that Mike would find an unpredictable crisis extremely stressful because of his high need for autonomy and independence.

As a result of this concern, a conference was arranged through which Mike was assisted by the caregivers to see that it is important for individuals to learn to trust the merits of an intervention or plan developed with professionals and derived from a core of tested scientific information. At the conclusion of the conference, each member (the nurse-educator, physician, and Mike) appeared satisfied that a positive outcome had been achieved. Especially satisfying had been the interactions among the three that seemed to demonstrate that Mike was able to share his concerns about his welfare. However, as Mike opened the door of the small conference room of the office suite, he turned his head and said, "I hope that I can depend on you and what you have just been saying for the last thirty minutes about trusting the pros to act in my best interests."

Passive-Ambivalent

The *passive-ambivalent strategy* is based on a combination of hostility toward others and a fear of social rejection and disapproval. The patient resolves this conflict by repressing his resentment. He overconforms and overcomplies on the surface; however, lurking behind this front of propriety and restraint are intense contrary feelings which, on rare occasion, seep through his controls. (Millon, 1969, p. 92)

STEPHAN

Stephan was considered "a good child" in the four-year-old group at the day care center. He was the oldest of three children in his two-parent family and spent six hours a day at the center because his mother had a six-month-old ill baby at home and his grandmother could not attend to more than one other child, his two-year-old sister. His mother helped him dress for the trip to the center each morning. Each time he started to object to his trip or to slam the door and awaken the baby, his mother gave him a hug and reminded him that he was being a big boy—almost like Daddy as he went off each day. Instead of resorting to tears, his lips quivered and he kissed his mother several times, rather than the customary once as he formerly did when he left home. In response, she placed small pieces of candy in his pocket.

At the center, he played normally with the other four-year-old boys. He always permitted them to share his toys, games, or treats at meal or break time. He appeared able and content to follow the rules. However, he seldom sat beside a girl or played in a unisex fashion with the girls in his group—even when other little boys he enjoyed as playmates did this or the teacher encouraged him to do so. Some of his submerged hostility (possibly caused by his sister's preferred position at home) emerged full force one afternoon, however, when the children prepared for their naps. Susan, a child whose relationship to him was neutral, had her cot collapse suddenly, entrapping her arm and causing her to cry loudly with pain. Several of the children cried with her or otherwise showed their concern at her hurt. Stephan behaved differently; he walked around in circles for several minutes and repeatedly called aloud, "That's what she gets. Always taking my place." The center health supervisor noted this, and after the appropriate care had been given to Susan, she asked the teacher if she could talk with him. Apparently, in his active response Stephan had released much pent-up anger which relaxed him greatly, because he was found asleep when the health supervisor reached his cot.

In a subsequent conference between the center health supervisor and Stephan's mother, the mother recalled that Stephan was unusually compliant most of the time. During a recent illness, however, the mother observed that Stephan was cooperative initially but later made sudden outbursts without observable provocation. The mother was not able to relate the attacks to the pain or discomfort of the illness or to the usual stressors faced by the ill child. Finally, the mother concluded this aspect of the discussion with the explanation that probably Stephan was so well-behaved because the outbursts were his safety valves; hence one could endure the sudden but brief changes in Stephan's behavior.

Active-Ambivalent

The *active-ambivalent strategy* represents an inability to resolve conflicts similar to those of the passive-ambivalent; however, these conflicts remain close to consciousness and intrude into everyday life. The individual gets himself into endless wrangles and disappointments as he vacillates between deference and conformity, at one time, and aggressive negativism, the next. His behavior displays an erratic pattern of explosive anger or stubborness intermingled with moments of hopeless dependency, guilt, and shame. (Millon, 1969, p. 92)

SARA

Sara represented a person of many moods to her contacts at work, school, and home. Usually, she was able to perform the expected tasks in these situations, that is, as an employee for three months in a busy clerical office job; part-time student in an evening education program; and cherished only daughter of an older-aged, upper lower-class family. However, she appeared to be caught up in storms of her own making because of her desire to be herself, to be her own person.

She performed the employment tests at a very high level; dressed in the usually acceptable manner for the initial interview and during the first month of employment; and otherwise engaged in exemplary office behavior during this period. However, the staff noted that later she was unable to complete her assignment acceptably and that her complaints about office decorum and procedures increased. She informed her peers that the office was operated in sexist fashion, that is, a male manager and all female staff; that conformity was an evil that inhibited creative achievement; and that change in this society had to come from the grassroots level. At the end of the second month, she decided to leave this work because it stifled her. However, the attitude of the manager in an evaluation changed her decision. As he reviewed her record, he noted her attendance at night school and encouraged her to remain on the staff because of her potential.

This conflict was a familiar one in that she was again placed in a position wherein she despised the conformity required by the establishment, rebelled, but because of the unexpected deference of the manager, was persuaded to remain as an employee. She confided to her parents that she was able to handle this personal crisis and the subsequent headaches because of her rationalization that whereas she was not the most productive employee, she was a valuable one, despite her rebelliousness at the system. Her parents appeared pleased, she related to a school advisor, that their daughter was "making her mark" at work and at school. Although the parents did not understand why their daughter tried so hard, they seemed to sanction her moody behavior at home because she was ambitious and "going places."

When Sara was ill with mononucleosis during a sudden outbreak of the disease at the college, she appeared to be engulfed in a new set of conflicts. This illness was an inconvenience to Sara, to say the least, because of her work and school obligations. These stressors seemed to provoke her to demonstrate anger regarding the diet, the need to rest, and the other general restrictions of illness. Nevertheless, Sara was compelled, because of the dependency produced by the illness, to conform to a regimen prescribed by the caregivers at the college infirmary. It appeared that her mother, as the primary helper in the home, was able to cope with the erratic angry behavior of her daughter because she had learned that this kind of behavior would quickly be followed by respites of passive ambivalence. To an observer, the behavior in the family was very stress-inducing, and was probably the consequence of long-standing patterns of interaction wherein each individual in the constellation was involved in an ongoing scenario directed to the needs of Sara.

The foregoing illustrations demonstrate that the eight strategies were initially used to relieve otherwise potentially untenable situations for the clients who employed them. However, their capacity for restricting, limiting, or crippling individual behavior, thereby encouraging maladaptation, was depicted in the narratives. For example, the consequences were reinforcing, thereby allowing the gains to become secondary reinforcers of behavior and further entrapping the individual in his or her position on the unhealthy end of the behavior continuum.

COPING WITH CRISIS

The goal of coping with a crisis is for the individual to return to the precrisis level of functioning or to function at a higher level following the crisis (Ewing, 1978). Caplan (1964) considered the coping behaviors associated with crisis situations and identified several which he termed *maladaptive* or *maladjustive*: "the evasion of crisis tasks, lack of activity in exploring the crisis situation, inability to express and to master negative feelings in consonance with the stress, or difficulty in obtaining help from others in handling feelings and in dealing with the crisis tasks" (p.83).

The individual who has a history of having seizures but .who refuses to take the anticonvulsive medication prescribed is evading the crisis task. Strategy for helping this individual cope might include exploring the reasons for his noncompliance, which could range from embarrassment to denial that, in fact, he has a problem. On the other hand, the health care provider could work on identifying effective reinforcers for taking the medication. The goal for the provider is to assist the client in performing the crisis task so that he can resume his former activities, with taking the medication being for him a minor adjustment in those activities. If in the process he gains some insight into his self-concept or he adjusts the priorities in his life so that his behavior is more adaptive, he will have reached a higher level of functioning as a result of the crisis.

A father who does not investigate the circumstances of his son's obvious change in behavior is exhibiting a lack of activity in exploring the crisis situation. Again, this failure to cope with the crisis may be motivated from any number of sources. The father may be frankly afraid of his son and his son's friends and fear the repercussions of any probing, or, he may just be denying that his son could be involved in any inappropriate behavior. Efforts to support the father in exploring his son's new behavior could lead to a solution of the immediate problem, whether treatment for the son's drug-related behavior or problem-solving of the young man's involvement with a burglary ring. If the results include better communication and respect between father and son, they both will have attained a higher level of functioning.

The inability to express and to master negative feelings related to the crisis is exemplified by nurses who refuse to acknowledge that certain patients are indeed difficult to serve. To deny the anger means that the nurse does not handle the situation adaptively. The nurse may change jobs or develop a physical illness to avoid being at work. By acknowledging angry feelings, the nurse may be able to obtain support from colleagues and make plans for dealing with the situation. Hopefully, the nurse will gain experience with problem-solving, and by being accepting of feelings will become a more effective nurse.

Clients who are identified as being chronically mentally ill typically have a particularly difficult time obtaining help from others. They may have been severely rebuffed in the past and prefer to have their needs unmet than to risk being refused help again. Another barrier to obtaining help may be the inability to articulate one's needs or to consider alternatives to one's current situation. The health care provider who is sensitive enough to offer acceptable help to a regressed client not only meets that client's immediate needs, but increases the possibility that the client will seek help in the future.

The individual in crisis may identify these difficulties himself or herself and seek help, or the individual may be identified by some helping person in the community as exhibiting maladaptive behaviors. Caregivers in the health delivery system are in a particularly good position to observe clients and determine whether their behaviors are appropriate or inappropriate. In the case of inappropriate behaviors, the caregiver can initiate intervention. If successful, the outcome will be relief of the current crisis, decreased probability of future crises, and restoration to the precrisis level or attainment of a higher level of functioning.

COPING AS A DEVELOPMENTAL PROCESS

Both Vaillant (1971) and Gazda (1971) have indicated that coping behaviors vary across developmental stages. Vaillant described differences in terms of "maturity," which meant that as people age they acquire more mature means of coping. For Vaillant, mature defenses were healthy defenses that he viewed as well-orchestrated composites of simpler mechanisms. These mature defenses emerged usually during adolescence and seemed to result from successful establishment of an identity. Vaillant considered defenses to be *maladaptive* if they led toward avoidance of conflict and unnecessary regression and if they impeded realistic gratification. He labelled them *adaptive* if they minimized regression and led toward eventual conflict resolution. It followed that if more mature mechanisms emerged as one developed, then coping behaviors that were adaptive at one stage of development might be maladaptive at a later stage of development. Gazda identified the coping behaviors that are appropriate for each stage of development and suggested that these behaviors may be used as a means of evaluating individuals. Failure to exhibit the behaviors appropriate for one's developmental level was indicative of some maladaptive behavior.

In order to facilitate healthy coping behaviors in other individuals, caregivers must be aware of the different psychological structures along the developmental continuum from the infant to the aged individual. Lazarus (1966) pointed out that important details of psychological stress production and reduction will be different at these developmental levels. Motives and techniques available for coping vary—as do fundamental resources and the nature of the coping processes—depending upon whether one is dealing with an infant, young child, or mature adult. Gazda (1971) identified coping behaviors that correspond with developmental tasks during preschool and early school, preadolescent, and adolescent and adult periods.

Developmental Stages of Coping Behaviors

Biosocial-psychological coping behaviors of early childhood were identified by Gazda (1971) as adjusting to less private attention; developing the ability to give affection; learning to share attention; beginning to develop the ability to interact with age-mates; adjusting in the family to the expectations the family has for the child as a member of the social unit; developing the ability to take directions and to be obedient in the presence of authority; developing the ability to be obedient in the absence of authority, where conscience substitutes for authority; learning to identify with adult male and female roles; adjusting to expectations from one's improving muscular abilities; developing sex modesty; developing large muscle control; learning to coordinate large muscles and small muscles; meeting adult expectations for restrictive exploration and manipulation of an expanding environment; improving one's use of the symbol system; elaborating on the concept of pattern; and developing a genuine notion about one's place in the cosmos.

According to Gazda (1971), during late childhood individuals must cope with freeing themselves from primary identification with adults; learning to give as much love as they receive; clarifying the adult world as over and against the child's world; establishing peer group ties and learning to belong; learning more rules and developing true morality; beginning to identify with social contemporaries of the same sex; refining and elaborating skill in the use of small muscles; learning more realistic ways of studying and controlling the physical world; learning to use language to exchange ideas and to influence listeners; beginning to understand real causal relations; and developing a scientific approach.

Gazda (1971) included persons aged nine through 13 as preadolescents. Coping behaviors preadolescents must develop include establishing independence from adults in all areas of behavior; accepting oneself as a worthwhile person worthy of love; behaving in accordance with a shifting peer code; reasserting and extending rules and principles related to controlling one's emotions; identifying with one's sex mates; recognizing one's thoughts and feelings about one's self in the face of significant body changes and their concomitants; accepting the reality of one's appearance; controlling and using a "new body"; perfecting skills of getting around the city and elsewhere; using language to express and to clarify more complex concepts; moving from the concrete to the abstract; and applying general principles to the particular.

Late adolescents (ages 15 to 17) cope with their environment by establishing themselves as independent individuals in a mature way; building a mutual bond with a (possible) marriage partner; adopting an adult-patterned set of social values by learning a new peer code; learning to verbalize contradictions in moral codes as well as discrepancies between principle and practice and resolving these problems in a responsible manner; exploring possibilities for a future mate and acquiring "desirability"; choosing an occupation; preparing to accept one's role in manhood or womanhood as a responsible citizen of the larger community; learning appropriate outlets for sex drives; improving motor skills through exercise and practice while achieving as much body poise and grace as one probably ever will have; possibly devoting one's life to discovering better ways of understanding and controlling phenomena in the physical world; achieving the level of reasoning of which one is able; and formulating a workable belief and value system.

Early adulthood was delineated by Gazda (1971) as being from ages 18 to 30 with coping behaviors including applying the rules appropriate to one's social class in selecting a mate; learning to control and express feelings; achieving biological sexual satisfaction; accepting the role of parent, adjusting to a reduction of sex life during pregnancy; making psychological adjustment to first pregnancy; participating in adult education courses directed to one's needs; meeting the physical and emotional needs of one's young child; learning to adapt daily and weekly schedules to the needs of the child; furnishing and managing the house; succeeding in one's occupation; learning what is expected of one in civic organizations such as lodges, clubs, and churches; adapting to social pressure for civic participation or preparing to participate in labor unions and fraternal orders; forming a leisure time pattern and finding others to share it; and selecting among several alternative congenial groups to join.

Ages 30 to 55 years incorporate the middle age, and Gazda (1971) identified the coping behaviors for this age as adjusting to heavy professional or vocational demands on the individual's time by civic and social groups; filling the void of children leaving home; maintaining a satisfactory economic standard of living; providing good role models for one's adolescent children; giving freedom and guidance to one's teenagers as well as one's nephews and nieces; abandoning most strenuous forms of leisure time activities while developing those activities that are meaningful and satisfying and applicable to middle and old age; taking action necessary to achieve those life-long ambitions that may require a rather high degree of financial stamina and financial expenditures; refocusing on role as wife or husband; providing support and understanding for one's spouse; maintaining one's personal attractiveness and charm; accepting the decline in physical activity and aging of the body; adjusting to changing moods and sexual activities; and working out affectionate but independent relationships with aging parents.

The age of later maturity is from 55 upward, and the following coping behaviors of that age were identified by Gazda (1971): adjusting to diminishing physical strength induced by cardiovascular and other ailments; adjusting to increased leisure time activity and part-time employment; adjusting expenditures to reduced income; dealing with loss of one's spouse; learning to participate in old-age groups; exerting leadership in political and civic groups; and adjusting to a changing physical environment, as in an apartment in a complex for the aging or in the home of a child or other relative.

COPING BEHAVIORS AND GOALS

One way of determining whether a particular behavior is successful or unsuccessful is to decide whether or not it achieved the goal for which it was intended. However, *successful* doesn't always equal *adaptive*, as can be seen in Table 3-1, where it is noted that the price of the coping behavior might be higher than expected. This situation may occur when an individual has an allergic reaction to an antibiotic. The infection may be controlled (that is, the goal reached) but the behavior may not have been adaptive (that is, the maximization of the chances of the survival of the individual).

In spite of the recognized limitations, goal achievement—in a significant number of cases—is a useful criterion for determining the effectiveness of coping behaviors. This principle is true for the unconscious defense mechanisms as well as for conscious coping behaviors. This has implications for those in the health-related professions because catastrophic illnesses may be overwhelming to clients and their families if they try to comprehend the whole realm of implications at one time (Mechanic, 1974). In such a situation, the mechanism of denial may be useful and adaptive in alleviating some of the initial pain (Moos & Tsu, 1977). On the other hand, if the denial is used to the extent that the patient refuses to undergo life-saving

TABLE 3-1.
CLASSIFICATION OF COPING BEHAVIORS

	Conscious	Unconscious
Adaptive	Behaviors are adequate for alleviating or attenuating the correctly identified threat or its consequences.	Behaviors are unconscious temporarily so that the individual can maintain his or her equilibrium until solution is possible.
		Behaviors are used temporarily to relieve pain and distress until facts can be faced.
Maladaptive	Behaviors are "too little too late" or inappropriate for the threat; the threat is underestimated; the price is higher than expected.	Unconscious behaviors are used habitually so that reality is not tested and the individual's needs are not met and realistic pleasures are missed.

surgery, the denial is no longer serving a useful purpose, for in the long run the goals of the individual will not be met. So denial in the latter case would be maladaptive. In fact, according to Vaillant (1971), denial is rarely adaptive in adults.

Sometimes the affective response to coping, even though the coping behaviors were successful, occurs after the threat has been eliminated or avoided. Lazarus (1966) gave an example of such a reaction:

> The driver makes a rapid judgment concerning a crash, and brakes, steers, or engages in some other maneuver to avoid impact, all with seeming coolness and control. After the danger is over, he becomes extremely apprehensive and perhaps so tremulous or faint that he must stop for a time to 'get hold of himself.'. . . Quite different psychological processes are involved in the various stages of the psychological-stress reaction. One possibility rests on the assumption that the type of reaction noted above seems to occur in the context of an accident in which the danger

emerges fairly suddenly and is over in a comparatively short time. The individual must take direct coping action, sometimes of a fairly complex sort. . . . Only coordinated and concerted attention to the coping maneuver succeeds in preventing catastrophe. The interpretation is, therefore, that attention is deployed entirely to the actions that are necessary so that full cognitive elaboration of the consequences of failure to prevent the harmful confrontation is not permitted . . . after the danger has passed, the full significance of what has or could have happened unfolds. It is then that the terrible consequences are fully assimilated. (p. 42)

The caregivers in the health setting must be aware of such postcrisis reactions and be prepared to intervene when necessary. This is seen particularly in cases of major elective surgery where the patient consciously faces high risk of death before surgery, prepares for death, and then lives.

Ables (1973) presented a case of a woman who exemplifies the maladaptive coping behavior of evading the task.

Mrs. X had been seen with her husband in marital therapy for several months. Her history was marked by a previous unsuccessful marriage and a tumultuous life. She had had two previous hospitalizations, the latter of which included electroconvulsive shock therapy. Mrs. X reacted to stresses by periodic aborted efforts at trying to leave her present husband, by being chronically fatigued, by suffering with various physical symptoms, and by heavy doses of drugs, both to sleep and to escape when situations became unbearable. The immediate events that led up to her suicidal attempt and hospitalization involved an out-of-town trip in an effort to get child support from her former husband. While she was away from her family, Mrs. X "cheated" on her husband, became involved with a drug pusher, and from her own account behaved in such an incorrigible way that she alienated friends and family, reaping for herself boundless feelings of guilt and shame. Hospitalization was seen as contributing to Mrs. X's pattern of avoiding threatening situations.

Bard and Sutherland (1955) studied the adaptation of 20 women to radical mastectomies. This study exemplified several aspects of coping: the patients' coping behaviors at the first sign of a lump or change in the breast, the patients' coping behaviors with regard to the surgery, the postoperative period, and rehabilitation. Additional coping behaviors were examined as the patients' behaviors toward their husbands and other people were explored. Then the husbands' attitudes were considered. All of these coping behaviors ran the gamut from healthy to unhealthy. Some women initially denied the symptoms and put off seeking medical attention for six months or more. Others sought medical attention without delay, but Bard and Sutherland warned that denial may have been operating still even in those women who did seek early help. Some women had been able to express their fear of anesthesia and of surgery, the fear of not waking up, and the fear of being disfigured; others denied that they had been told that a mastectomy was a possibility before surgery. Coping behaviors during the immediate postoperative period included return to extreme dependency on their mothers and anger expressed toward the surgeons and nurses. Sexual relations were difficult or impossible for some women following surgery. Some husbands were supportive; others were resentful and unresponsive.

Cancer and the surgical procedures implemented to control it are devastating, but they occur frequently. It is imperative that the caregivers identify the coping behaviors being used and facilitate the clients' rehabilitation by helping them to adjust to perhaps an altered body and a different way of life.

SUPPORT SYSTEMS

An important variable in the assessment of an individual's coping abilities is the adequacy of his or her support systems. According to the studies by Caplan (1974) of individual responses during crisis, the outcome is influenced not only by the current ego strength of the individual, but also—and perhaps more importantly—by the quality of the emotional support and task-oriented assistance provided by the social network within which that individual grapples with the crisis event. Caplan defined a support system as an "enduring pattern of continuous or intermittent ties that play a significant part in maintaining the psychological and physical integrity of the individual over time" (1974, p. 7). Health care professionals are part of the support systems used by individuals, and Caplan was particularly perceptive in his identification of the role that nurses can play as primary care providers in the emerging concept of community mental health.

Caplan's (1974) writing on the importance of support systems is in agreement with the view expressed by Cassel (1974). Based on data obtained from animal studies, Cassel derived four principles that he believed to be worth considering in the identification of factors contributing to mental illness in humankind. The first is the suggestion that "in human populations the circumstances in which increased susceptibility to disease would occur would be those in which, for a variety of reasons, individuals are not receiving any evidence (feedback) that their actions are leading to desirable and/or anticipated consequences" (p. 405). The second principle is that "not all members of a population are equally susceptible to the effects of these social processes. . . . the high levels of blood pressure found in American blacks, who not only usually occupy a subordinate position in society but whose lives are frequently characterized by considerable evidence of social and familial disorganization" may be evidence that individuals in subordinate position may be more susceptible to effects of stress (p. 406). The third principle is concerned with the available protective factors, those devices that buffer or cushion the individual from the physiological or psychological consequences of disorganization—both biological and social (p. 407). The final principle relates to the manifestations of ill health that might be anticipated under conditions of social change and disorganization (p. 407). These and other data strongly suggest that both mental and physical diseases have multiple causes and an individual's coping ability may be a very important factor in determining whether or not the individual escapes illness.

SOME DETERRENTS TO ACCURATE ASSESSMENT OF CLIENTS' COPING STRATEGIES

It is not easy to identify the coping behaviors a patient is employing. In fact, the process that would appear to be the easiest is the most difficult and the most crucial. As Marriner (1979) suggested, lack of skill in observation and faulty listening habits are major reasons for failing to understand a client. Other deterrents mentioned by Marriner are erroneous interpretations, value statements, cliches, automatic responses, reliance upon patterned approaches, stereotypes, preconceptions, labeling, consideration of facts in isolation, inadequate consideration of social and cultural factors, treating the patient as an object, and a lack of good intention on the part of the nurse.

ASSESSMENT OF CLIENTS' COPING STRATEGIES

Identification of the coping behaviors of clients by nurses and other caregivers can be facilitated by the use of observational skills and an assessment tool, which enables the caregiver to obtain the essential information in a systematic fashion. Information should also be gathered by a second observer, and it can be more readily contrasted with that of the first assessor through the use of comparable systematic methods of information gathering.

Occasionally caregivers do not recognize unhealthy coping strategies—ones that portend to become maladaptive behavior and therefore limit the growth or functional possibilities of an individual. The use of an assessment instrument would assist the caregivers in the identification of inappropriate behavior measures used characteristically by the client to cope with stressors or threats. Two models are suggested here that may be useful to the caregiver in detecting the coping strategies employed by clients (Figures 3-2 and 3-3). Inherent in their use,

COPING STRATEGY ASSESSMENT TOOL #1

1. Name of client

2. Residence

3. Sex   4. Age   5. Marital Status

6. Children or older residents in the home (number and ages)

7. Children away from home

8. Living arrangement (single or multiple dwelling)

9. Identifiable disabilities

   Physical

   Emotional

10. Overall health status

11. Long-standing events/Recent crises or changes of life pat-
    tern (hospitalization, change of residence, family group
    alterations, change of job, change of income, change of
    school, other changes as deemed significant)

12. Reason for encounter with caregiver or service

13. Identification of the stressor(s).

FIGURE 3-2. Assessment tool #1.

14. Identification/description of the antecedent stimuli.

15. Identification/description of the setting for the interview/ observation.

16. Description of the client: his/her appearance.

17. Relationship of any resource person involved.

18. Description of the coping strategy.

19. Identification/description of the reinforcers that influence the use of the strategy.

20. Assessment of the potential merit of the strategy for goal achievement and eventual healthy or unhealthy adaptation.

Initial Assessment	Followup Assessment

21. Recommendation for follow-through with the client.

22. Name and role of the assessor_____

FIGURE 3-2 (continued).

COPING STRATEGIES ASSESSMENT TOOL #2

Personal Characteristics

1. Name

2. Age

3. Residence

4. Sex

5. Children or older residents in the home (number and ages)

6. Marital status

7. Living arrangement (single or multiple dwelling, or special characteristic)

8. Identifiable disabilities

9. Overall health status

10.

Long-standing significant events/recent crisis	Coping behavior	Coping strategy	Antecedent events	Validation	Outcome of strategy used

11. Name and role of the assessor_____

FIGURE 3-3. Assessment Tool #2.

122

however, is the recommendation that more than one sample of the behavior be made; that another observer validate the findings; and that another kind of assessment (narrative, other) augment the assessment tool in order to reduce the possibility of judgment-making based on "the single observation."

Chapter 4

Implications for Intervention

In this chapter several models for intervention are presented (see Figure 4-1). Discussions and guidelines for the application of crisis intervention theory, counseling, and counterconditioning and other approaches emanating from concepts of learning theory are included. Several methods deemed helpful in the elimination of maladaptive behaviors and the development and strengthening of healthy coping patterns in clients who have a diversity of case histories are presented. *When to intervene, with whom,* and *how* are critical questions that health care providers must raise and answer. Although there are no foolproof formulas, there are guidelines that should be explored and evaluated.

INTERVENTION IN CRISIS

A crisis is a time for change; it is a turning point. Morgan and Moreno (1973) divided crises into two categories: Developmental crises are universal critical transition points including birth, adolescence, marriage, aging, and death; coincidental crises occur at random in peoples' lives and include accidents, natural disasters, and illnesses. Burgess and Lazare (1976) made the same division but labeled the parts internal or maturational crises of the life cycle and external or situational crises. Pittman (in Langsley & Kaplan, 1968) stated that in order to resolve the crisis there must be a definition of what is going on and of what changes are indicated, and then those changes must be made. If crises seem to occur frequently in a family or with an individual, it may be necessary to identify the stressors and any factors that make the person or family crisis-prone. The goal of crisis intervention, according to Aguilera and Messick (1974), is to return the client to his or her previous level of functioning or possibly to a higher level with greater capacity for problem-solving.

Identifying the Problem

As shown in Figure 4-1, a crisis is precipitated when a threat or stressor is perceived in the individual's environment. Ap-

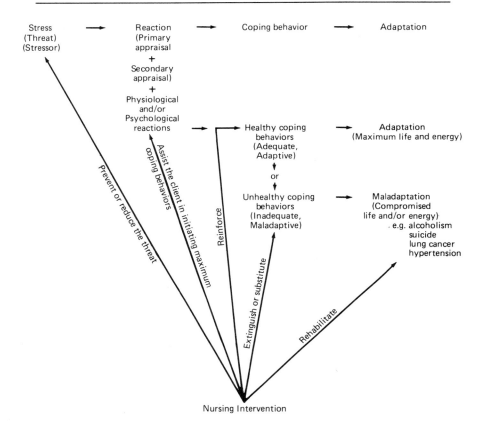

FIGURE 4-1. Model for nursing intervention in the coping process.

praisals are made, the primary appraisal being the perception of the threat by the individual and the secondary appraisal being the decision of what to do about the threat. The situation is not defined as a crisis until the strategies decided upon do not relieve the anxiety of the individual. At this point, the helper must identify the problem as the client sees it and clarify with the client the ineffective solutions that the client has been attempting. The problem may appear different to the client than to the helper. For example, an 85-year-old diabetic woman who was recently found unconscious in her room at a home for the aged defines her problem as loneliness; the nurse defines it as noncompliance to a diabetic diet, as the client has been spending her days munching on candy while she watches television. If the nurse listens to the client and initiates intervention aimed at relieving the client's loneliness, the probability of getting the client to adhere to an appropriate diet will be increased. The first step in crisis intervention is, therefore, the identification of the problem from the client's perspective.

Choosing the Best Alternative

The second step in crisis intervention is to help the client choose the best of alternatives and implement the choice. Alternatives for the elderly diabetic lady include moving her to a more controlled environment where nursing personnel can make sure that she takes her Orinase and eats only the three prescribed meals at regular times each day; she could be encouraged to cooperate, and her preference for certain foods could be considered in planning meals with her; she could be persuaded to move into the house with her son and his family so that they could be responsible for her; or she could be just left alone to "take her chances," for after all, eating is about the only pleasure she has left.

Choosing the best alternative is not often simple, the possible outcomes of the various choices must be thought through. If the elderly lady is placed in a controlled environment, there may be some assurance that she will take her medication and be served an adequate diet; but what about the quality of life? What about the individual's dignity? Some data have been interpreted to indicate that confining an individual against his or her wishes may contribute to an early, unexpected death. Involving the client in the choice of alternatives to be implemented is clearly indicated. Also, the needs and preferences of others must be considered.

Evaluating and Terminating

The third step in crisis intervention is evaluation and termination. The caregiver reviews with the patient what happened or what the problem was, what was done about it, and what the outcome was. It is possible that the alternative chosen was not the best one and further adjustments must be made. Perhaps the best alternative was chosen; then the task is to understand why it worked so that the client's problem-solving skills can be reinforced. Sometimes evaluation results in beginning the cycle again.

Some crises can be anticipated, and planning for them can prevent great emotional upheavals at the time of the actual event. For example, elective surgery can be anticipated by giving the client instructions about what is expected of the client and what can be expected to happen. The individual can be told how much pain to expect and where, but assured that medication or other aids will be available to relieve it. Other information may include what tubes will be found attached upon awakening from the anesthesia. The client will be more likely to cooperate without fear if told before surgery that instructions will be given to cough, sit up, lie still, and so forth following surgery. Janis (1974) labeled this precrisis preparation "emotional innoculation."

INTERVENTION USING ROY'S ADAPTATION MODEL

Another plan of intervention has been developed by Sister Calista Roy. The Roy Adaptation Model is primarily a systems model with interactionist levels of analysis within it (Galbreath, 1980; Roy, 1980). This model is based on the following eight assumptions:

1. The person is a bio-psycho-social being. 2. The person is in constant interaction with a changing environment. Daily experience supports this assumption. One need only cite the vicissitudes of the weather, or of traffic conditions, as examples. The person confronts constant physical, social, and psychologic changes in his environment and is continually interacting with these. 3. To cope with a changing world, the person uses both innate and acquired mechanisms, which are biologic, psychologic, and social in origin.

4. Health and illness are one inevitable dimension of the person's life. 5. To respond positively to environmental changes, the person must adapt. 6. The person's adaptation is a function of the stimulus he is exposed to and his adaptation level. The person's adaptation level is determined by the combined effect of three classes of stimuli: (1) focal stimuli, or stimuli immediately confronting the person, (2) contextual stimuli or all other stimuli present, and (3) residual stimuli, such as beliefs, attitudes, or traits which have an indeterminate effect on the present situation. 7. The person's adaptation level is such that it comprises a zone which indicates the range of stimulation that will lead to a positive response. If the stimulus is within the zone, the person responds positively. However, if the stimulus is outside the zone, the person cannot make a positive response. 8. The person is conceptualized as having four modes of adaptation: physiologic needs, self-concept, role function, interdependence relations. (Roy, 1980, pp. 180-182)

The goal of action within this model is the person's adaptation in these four adaptive modes. (Roy, 1974, p. 183)

A group of students undertook to test the Roy Adaptation Model in clinical settings (Wagner, 1976). Although there was some difficulty expressed in the implementation of the model in the intensive care unit, the positive findings reported included the holistic view of the patient provided by considering the four modes of adaptation and the fact that the model emphasized the patient's positive as well as negative behaviors. The difficulties in implementing the model were that it "would take considerable dedication, education, and personal commitment to this model of nursing for it to function effectively in most nursing service situations" (Wagner, 1976, p. 685).

Brower and Baker (1976) used the Roy Adaptation Model as a conceptual model for a geriatric nurse practitioner program and found that this model provided "the necessary framework to give direction to practitioner education;" offered "a relevant way of viewing the older adult in relation to his environment;" and delineated "guidelines for nurse practitioner action," (p. 689). Miller and Hellenbrand (1981) have incorporated Roy's Model in an eclectic approach to practice.

INTERVENTION USING SUPPORTIVE TECHNIQUE (MILLON)

There are times when an individual is in a situation in which the outcome is predictably going to be tragic. A patient dying of cancer, a parent whose child is dying of leukemia or a brain tumor, or a nurse who is caring for a dying patient are examples of such individuals. In such cases, given that the coping behaviors being exhibited are appropriate, the most effective action on the part of the caregiver and other members of the situation would be to provide support. Support involves the patient himself or herself and focuses on strengthening coping behaviors of the individual. Support incorporates the procedures of ventilation, reassurance, and persuasion (Millon, 1969).

Sympathetic listening on the part of the caregiver allows and encourages the client or patient to ventilate feelings. Getting things off their chests without fear of reproach is a luxury many individuals do not have but would find extremely beneficial. It is not necessary for the care provider to probe or make the patient reveal or talk about matters he or she is not yet willing to express; the care provider must just be sure that verbalization by the client of thoughts or feelings needing to be expressed is not cut off.

Reassurance should not be given to the patient who needs to identify and explore his fears: Will the patient experience pain? Will the patient's family be permitted to stay with him or her? The caregiver must, of course, be honest and sometimes may have to say "I don't know, but I'll find out," or "We can't be sure in your case, but someone will be with you."

Persuasion takes the form of encouraging the person to do what he or she can to help in the situation as much as possible. In order to maintain some independence, the person may be persuaded to do things for himself or herself for as long as possible that are adequate to meet maintenance or therapeutic needs. A mother may be persuaded to bathe and care for her terminally ill child in order to reassure her of her worth as a mother, but she should not be urged or forced to do something she is not emotionally or physically able to do.

INTERVENTION USING THE CLIENT'S COPING STRATEGIES

Using the eight coping strategies described by Millon (1969) and summarized in Chapter 3, consider the various reactions one might encounter from a mother of a malformed newborn. Also, think about the possible interventions that would appear to be most appropriate in each situation.

Passive-Detached

The mother who has a pattern of using passive-detached strategies might act as though she were merely observing what is happening to her and her baby; she may express little emotion or concern for herself or for her family. Primarily, the nurses should be supportive, which includes being attentive and responding to any requests, even if only to explain a delay or to suggest an alternative. It is important to give this mother factual information, but not to push her to respond or probe into her feelings, for these individuals do not readily form close relationships.

Active-Detached

The mother who uses active-detached coping strategies will be even more difficult to help, for she will appear to distrust others and will actively place distance between herself and others. She may blame the doctors, nurses, her husband, or others for the malformation of her child. In order to provide care for mothers using this type of strategy, the nurse must be sure that any trust that is established is not betrayed by the nurse's failure to keep promises made to her. For example, any commitment such as to obtain another pain relieving medication for her or to provide her with the attending physician's office telephone number should be expediently implemented. The nurse should support the patient as much as she can tolerate, but the nurse should not push or probe. Instead, the nurse's best strategy is to listen and respond.

Passive-Dependent

The mother who uses a passive-dependent strategy will latch onto anyone who will provide support. At the same time, she may be very suggestible, so that a hint for her to think about something may take on an absolute quality. It is obviously necessary for the nurse to be careful about any explanations given the mother about her baby's condition or about any predictions about what she might expect to happen considering her baby's condition. This mother may be ingratiating or she may cry frequently and profusely. She will try almost anything to be "taken care of," she may want to be taken care of by everyone including her husband, her mother, her doctor, and her nurse. This client meets some of the needs of health care providers who need to be needed, for she does demonstrate appreciation. However, after the caregiver has listened, comforted, and spent considerable time with this patient, she will still want more, so limits must eventually be set. If structure is imposed gently but consistently from the beginning of the relationship, it might prevent, to some extent, the difficulties that may eventually arise as the patient demands more than the care provider is able or willing to give.

Active-Dependent

Casual observation of the mother who uses an active-dependent strategy may be deceiving, for this person tends to appear outgoing and independent while hiding her underlying fear of autonomy and her intense need for affection. It is likely that this mother's motivation for having a baby was so that she could please others. In this, she probably envisioned an adorable little rose-cheeked, doll-like infant that she could dress elaborately and evoke unending praise and admiration. The realities of being confronted with a child with a congenital defect will be difficult for her to grasp. She may refuse to accept the facts and make such comments as "Oh, everything is going to be all right," or "Oh, don't worry, Dr. X will take care of everything." The nurses can best approach this mother by commenting on her real strengths and support. For example, without being overly reassuring and thereby blocking therapeutic communication, the nurse might explore with the mother ways that her husband is supportive and how proud he appears to be of the way she is managing. Needless to say, the nurse's encouragement must be appropriately based on reality, for unfounded compliments tend to be more destructive than helpful and often lead to later distrust.

Passive-Independent

The mother who employs a passive-independent strategy tends to overvalue her own self-worth, and may, therefore, be rather shaken by being told that she has, in a sense, produced an imperfect child. She may interpret this event as a reflection of her own imperfection, which she may have a difficult time accepting. This mother may demand confirmation of the diagnosis by the "top authority" in the field, and even then she may not accept it. The nurse would do well to be prepared to be ignored; this way, the nurse may avoid having her own feelings ruffled or carrying a "chip" on her shoulder, for she will realize that the mother is merely employing a learned coping strategy that has worked for her in the past. The nurse may be most helpful by being patient, listening, and sending in the nursing supervisor or director of nurses whenever possible to help to rebuild this mother's self-esteem. The expertise of the nursing supervisor is not actually needed, but this mother will be impressed by titles. This mother's husband is going to need extra support also because his wife will be making numerous demands of him.

Active-Independent

The mother who uses an active-independent strategy is a real challenge. The nurse will not need to call in the nursing supervisor for her, because the mother will have summoned her already. She will aggressively seek information and authority figures, which is a manifestation of her indiscriminate striving for power. However, this mother will tend to reject others because they cannot be trusted, and since she cannot trust them she will "give orders" rather than seek the untrustworthy advice or opinions of others. The nurse must be prepared for the "put-down," for this mother will challenge her credentials as well as the credentials of the other specialists who are consulted. She may dismiss those who are trying to help her and call in others.

The nurse's goal is to try to assist the mother to re-establish her self-worth. The nurse can point out reality to this mother; for example, "Dr. X has performed more than 300 operations similar to the one he is suggesting for your son. I have cared for many of these babies following surgery and they are usually ready to go home in ten to fourteen days after the surgery. Would you like for me to arrange another conference with Dr. X before your decision is final?" Any tangible evidence of competence might be helpful, such as newspaper or journal articles about the physician or even about the condition and correction prescribed for her baby.

Passive-Ambivalent

The mother who uses a passive-ambivalent strategy is complicated because she is basically hostile toward others but at the same time afraid of social rejection and disapproval. This mother may be angry because she followed the doctor's orders carefully during her entire pregnancy, even though it entailed numerous sacrifices. Further, she states that she ate exactly the right kinds of food and may even have weighed her food to make sure that everything was correct. Then, how could this terrible thing have happened to her baby? Her life otherwise is orderly and controlled, and now something outside her control has happened. The nurse might help by encouraging this mother to re-establish control in any areas in which this is possible. Let her choose her food and when she wants to eat, if it is not contraindicated. Give her a schedule of events, or better, help her outline a reasonable and workable routine upon which she can rely. The nurse should be aware of the possibility of angry outbursts from this mother and should be tolerant and accepting, with the goal of helping the mother regain control of her own life and get back into a comfortable routine.

Active-Ambivalent

Erratic behavior will be exhibited by the mother who uses an active-ambivalent strategy. Sometimes she will be explosive, angry, and stubborn; often these aggressive behaviors are mingled with moments of hopeless dependency, guilt, and shame. The nurse can be most helpful by recognizing that this mother will anticipate negative events before such events occur. This is why she will sometimes appear angry and "take it out" on the nurse when there is no apparent reason for an outburst. To decrease the pressures of the environment as much as possible, the nurse should respond to the client's mood. For example, the nurse can structure the client and point out reality when the client is being explosive, or support and listen when the client is expressing some of her disappointments. However, the nurse should not let the client be unduly self-derogatory, because she may tend to be impulsive, and suicide is a danger. Mental health consultation should be sought immediately if the client makes a suicidal threat or gesture.

INTERVENTION USING COUNSELING TECHNIQUES

If assisting others to attain goals that are important to them is a function of the helping relationship (Brammer, 1977), health care providers are responsible for directly or indirectly teaching clients to cope. This responsibility includes offering assistance as indicated by the problem, including assessing the present level of coping ability of the client and his or her ability to identify realistic goals; to explore the options available; to facilitate the testing of the chosen option(s); and to evaluate the outcome in terms of personal and/or social satisfactions obtained. The direct coping assistance and subsequent feedback should enable clients to help themselves as well as others to cope. In order to teach clients coping behavior such as problem-solving and decision-making, assertiveness, parenting, family enrichment, stress management, creativity through divergent thinking, or dealing with many of the learned maladaptive behaviors, nurses and other care providers need the skills requisite to the tasks.

The acquisition of helping skills has been grounded in counseling theory. Two prominent approaches today differ but are not incongruent. Rogers (1957) proposed that the helping skills grew from helping attitudes. Simplistically stated, the skills grew from the attitudes of caring, regard, empathy, and realness (genuinness and sincerity) more readily than from the attitudes of so-called objectivity.

The other view emphasized the importance of learned, systematically applied helping behaviors in the form of combinations (Carkhuff & Berenson, 1976; Ivey, 1972; Kagan, 1975) in addition to the demonstration of the helping attitudes. These combinations of behaviors acquired by caregivers consisted primarily of attending and responding to client cues, verbal and nonverbal. For example, noting particular behavior, such as the repetitions, constrictions, or avoidance of terms, content, or descriptions of actions, thoughts, or feelings as well as signals from body language in the form of posture, mannerisms, and eye contact of the client provides useful information for the care provider. The care provider may explore the information further for correctness and check its validity with other information in order to respond helpfully.

Gazda (1973) referred to the acquirable skills as perceiving and responding in order to improve the primary vehicle of communication, one with important linkages in the vast human behavior network. Since many of the interpersonal difficulties of clients emerge from communication dysfunction, the attention to it should increase their coping effectiveness in the areas cited above, that is, problem-solving, decision-making, assertiveness, parenting, family enrichment, stress management, creativity through divergent thinking, and other forms of interaction. Although the care provider may not be expected to offer a package of skills requisite to proficiency in the areas cited, the effectiveness of counseling may be extended through the appropriate use of referrals to bibliotherapy, programmed instruction, workshops, short courses, interactional groups, or seminars as part of the counseling function.

Differences in counseling technique may emanate from the preferences of the counselor for behavior modification in contrast to the use of open-ended counseling with the client-established options as mechanisms for attainment of goals. Note that goals exist in the use of each technique or approach, and are usually mutually identified. This collaboration between the counselor and the client may enable the client to increase independence while accepting personal responsibility for action as well as outcome.

Deductive Model

Getz (1974) described a deductive model of counseling. In this model, the client and counselor develop perceptions of the conflict situation with the presentation of a series of themes. The counselor and client connect these themes, then isolate and prioritize the major themes. Subsequently, the client assumes the primary responsibility for the identification of the options available for resolving the conflict or crisis. Finally, a realistic plan is developed with the client as a major participant, and the plan is implemented and evaluated with the assistance of the counselor in terms of conflict (or crisis) resolution. The sequential review by the client and counselor of the elements in the counseling experience initiates the development of adaptive coping behavior that will be useful in the resolution of future conflicts—or possibly in the prevention of such problems. The following counselor-client situation illustrates the use of this model.

Ms. Bell, a 74-year-old retired teacher and widow, had been quite reluctant to move from her large but difficult-to-maintain older home in an inner-city location. She had moved into this setting as a bride, reared three sons in this house, and remained after the death of her husband 15 years ago. With the loss of Mr. Bell, Ms. Bell returned to teach in a small parochial school within walking distance from her home. To her children and friends her series of late life adjustments had been satisfactory. However, the encroachment of industry, traffic, noise, and the changes in the dwellings (from single family to multifamily) had been annoying. In fact, when her sons suggested that she recover from a bout with influenza in the home of one son who lived in the suburbs and then remain with this family because she was not strong enough to resume teaching or housecare, she agreed almost immediately. She appeared to make this transition readily, also.

After six months, just as the family grew comfortable with its new member, Ms. Bell's son was transferred to a distant city. Her other sons lived out of state; therefore, decisions had to be made immediately. Ms. Bell seemed to be caught in the middle without much power as her children and daughters-in-law decided that her large home must be sold, including the furnishings and her lifetime of collections. Soon after, arrangements were made for Ms. Bell to move into a retirement facility.

This impending change appeared to create a new personality. Ms. Bell began to eat less, lose weight, speak less enthusiastically, and remain in her room more frequently than in the past. Not even the activities of her cherished grandchildren or the family dog interested her. Her reading materials remained by her bed, untouched. In desperation, her sons consulted the health services agency of the retirement facility for advice about the way in which this series of events had affected her. The nurse-counselor arranged to meet Ms. Bell alone for several sessions and later met with her family.

In the first session, the counselor established a relationship that enabled her to gather essential information about the present problem. She explored the client's perception of this particular set of circumstances and sought the different themes inherent in it. After obtaining a general understanding of the problem, the counselor was able to consolidate the themes and focus on the problem to be resolved. With Ms. Bell, the counselor verified several problems (moving again, giving up the newly constituted family, and the impending adjustments to new living arrangements). After mutual investigation, Ms. Bell and the counselor concluded that the central problem or crisis was actually, "How will Ms. Bell remain Ms. Bell with all of these changes?" Moreover, the earlier changes had been recalled vividly by the client in the conference, and the new ones she added only compounded the situation.

Following agreement on the central theme and problem, the counselor and client began the search for options that would resolve the difficulties. These constituted the plan of attack; that is, the ways considered feasible and appropriate to maintain the identity, integrity, and independence of Ms. Bell within the limitations of the situation. The limitations were identified as social (living among people of a varied age range but who shared her preference for companionship and interaction); economic (financial obligation that was realistic in terms of available resources); and psychobiologic (affording adequate stimulation tempered with restraint and supervision for her psychological, spiritual, and physiological needs).

Finally, Ms. Bell developed a plan that appeared pleasing to her and offered her optimal independence plus security. She was able to prioritize her options for living, which ranged from levels of care to location. After careful consideration, she was amenable to the selection of a living arrangement in which she had a one-bedroom apartment in a garden level setting with access to older-aged companionship of her preference within the retirement compound. However, she also could occasionally observe or visit with children and their parents at a nearby school and participate in the local community organizations. Further, the services through this selection of residence included a medical care plan, food services as needed, transportation, laundry, and provisions for heavy cleaning.

This development was not only satisfactory to Ms. Bell, the able designer, but to her family and the counselor, who planned to observe the actualization of the plan. The key that ensured success was probably the ability of the counselor to establish a credible relationship with the client; identify the themes, draw them together, and focus on a central problem; enable the client to be assistive and validate the conclusions; permit the client to identify her options, establish priorities, and explore the consequences; and actualize the goal itself. Each component of this endeavor was assistive in the maintenance of Ms. Bell as a person—one with integrity who was worthy of self-respect at this stage in her life.

THE CONTRACT IN THE COUNSELING RELATIONSHIP

Goodyear and Bradley (1980) recommended the use of the contract in counseling as a valid agreement to define or specify the nature of the counselor-client relationship and the goals of the particular helping process. However, these counselors suggested further that the contracting process may have advantages that are helpful as a therapeutic modality. In the collaborative processes that are inherent in the development of a mutually acceptable and realistic contract or agreement related to goals, mutual benefits for the participants are possible.

The mutual advantages as identified by Goodyear and Bradley are summarized here:

1. The client can be assisted to realize that the intent of the relationship is to effect a change, to resolve a conflict. Therefore, the nature of the relationship and the importance of achievable goals are serious and consequential business.

2. The contract facilitates monitoring by the participants through references at intervals to goal accomplishment.

3. The purpose of the counseling relationship can be established early, thereby ensuring some protection for participants. For example, the early establishment of purpose may not prevent any explorations into irrelevant areas of minor consequence, but it protects the initial goal-oriented investments of the participants if that is their desire.

4. The protection to the participants is mutual, ensuring each member of his or her particular rights and responsibilities.

5. The contractual process facilitates self-exploration for the client through the examination of the nature and extent of the problem or conflict as he or she shares the problem with another individual. Also shared are attitudes, values, and beliefs. The counselor benefits as the exploration progresses and the counselor assumes the facilitative, review, and summation functions. The processes of self-exploration and self-discovery enable the individual to explore and experience feelings, often undeveloped to this point; expand awareness; and

identify new aspects of life. This includes the recognition of new options (Kahn & Greenberg, 1980).

Additionally, advocates believe that the successful application of this method depends on the skill of the counselor in the promotion of collaboration; the willingness for each participant to contract for realistic goals; and the recognition of individual motivational differences in clients. For example, distance may exist between what the client should do versus what the client wants to do. This reality must be dealt with by the participants in order to ensure that the goals will be ones that the client perceives as wanted, meaningful, achievable, and unimposed wherever possible. The rationale for this intent, in contrast to the selection of the "should-do," includes high generation of energy and motivation toward a much-wanted goal, perceived rewards for the goal achievement, and likelihood of acceptance of responsibility for outcomes by participants.

The contract as a therapeutic modality parallels the Carkhuff and Berensen (1977) model of helping, including the exploration phase. Further, the movement through the process enables the participants to progress from making decisions of purpose to recognizing counterpurposes ("I don't know if this is my real problem"); to discerning the meaning of the phenomenon ("I can't concentrate because. . . ."); to identifying what goal achievement will be ("I will be able to. . . ."); and to identifying the relationship of the purposes of the counseling interaction to the real wants of the client. An important part of the process includes the emergence of the client's perception that some of the payoffs of the achievement of new goals may mean the loss or limitation of other cherished intents. For example, the increased understanding that an individual obtains as an outcome of the identification of the payoffs may lead that participant to recognize that another payoff may be more realistic; more appropriate for the time, place, and persons involved; and capable of the generation of greater amounts of energy for action.

Although most caregivers realize that they assume important responsibilities when they employ counseling techniques to assist clients to modify behavior and increase or develop effective coping behavior, the importance of the counseling relationship in the selection of another kind of intervention and the introduction to other modes of therapy must be recognized. It is imperative, then, that care providers learn to practice appropriate counseling skills in order to establish therapeutic interactions that will increase the confidence of the client as he or she assists in the selection of an appropriate modality other than counseling itself as an intervention. Counseling, therefore, can be considered as an adjunct to other forms of intervention because it is the first step in a relationship model.

Increasingly, clients and caregivers have sought alternative ways of solving problems and dealing with the conflicts in their daily lives; hence the reemergence and development of group therapy and group participation as additional options designed to increase human potential. The succeeding discussion deals with the use of the small group as a mechanism for the development of adaptive coping behavior in clients in a therapeutic setting.

THE SMALL GROUP INTERACTION

The influence of the small group in the modification of the behavior of individual group members has been extensively documented (Benne & Levit, 1953; Lewin, 1951; Raven, 1969). The fact that humankind has lived and survived in formal and informal small groups has been undisputed historically. However, it was not until the late nineteenth and early twentieth centuries that the observations of sociologists, including Durkheim, Cooley, Mead, Simmel, and Tripplett (Knowles & Knowles, 1972), implicated small group interactional processes as responsible for important changes in the behavior of group members. Tripplett noted that a particular facilitating or "dynamogenic" effect occurred within groups which did not occur when individuals were alone. Later, Lewin's field theory postulated that a group exists in a fashion similar to an electro-magnetic field in physics in which the forces or variables affect group behavior.

As a consequence of these observations and postulations, some therapists and other devotees of group study foresaw the versatility of the small group in the potentiation of individual behaviors and personality development (Gazda, 1978; Lazarus 1975). Also, it was observed that small group interactions were able to increase the problem-solving and attentiveness behavior of its members. Ultimately, the verbal and nonverbal feedback as reinforcement from the group milieu would have profound effects on group participants. These possible effects included revisions and/or development of interactional skills, alterations of self-esteem or concept, and facilitation of the acquisition of adaptive coping behavior. Betz, Wilbur, and Roberts-Wilbur (1981) classified the major group modalities as the task-process, the socio-process, and the psycho-process group clusters, giving the distinguishing variables of each modality. Regardless of the modality chosen, the small group can be an effective instrument for increasing adaptive behavior in its members along several dimensions. As participation in the group heightens self-aware-ness and increases perception, for example, the involved in-dividuals may realize that their responsibilities for action and opportunities for risk-taking behavior increase. With the de-velopment of constructive interactive and related skills and the altered concept of the self, the person participating in a small group may eventually be able to incorporate these newly ac-quired behaviors into an overall more highly rewarding and/or acceptable way of performing in order to meet his or her goals and those of the larger society. The following situation may be useful in demonstrating this accomplishment.

Mr. Casper was a therapist responsible for the integration of daily living activities into the rehabilitation regimen of an organized group of male patients who had recently suffered a cerebral vascular ac-cident. Whereas Mr. Casper was exceedingly effective in his man-agement of the physical exercise program for these clients in the gymnasium, he expressed his frustration at their inability to continue an activity program without on-site direction despite the fact that their physio-psychosocial evaluations had implied that they were capable of initiating, performing, and completing certain tasks.

Although his clinical experience and training with this kind of client had been extensive, the therapist's age was at least three decades younger than that of the youngest client in this particular group. This fact was used often by the therapist to explain his lack of satisfactory follow-through with the group members. Finally, after a very frustrating group session, Mr. Casper invited a therapist familiar with group counseling techniques to visit this group at its next postexercise meeting in order to note the regressed behavior of the members. Instead of regressed behavior as the primary problem, the visiting therapist observed that clients with many abilities but certain physical limitations—which retraining would probably overcome—were defensive toward Mr. Casper.

Age disparity, then, did not appear to be of importance. In fact, when clients failed to report that they had performed the necessary physical activity or to demonstrate their increased strength and coordination, they were admonished by Mr. Casper in the group with comments that tended to increase their defensive behavior. For example, one client failed to perform the prescribed lifting exercises to strengthen the muscles of his lower extremity. After testing for progress by the therapist, he was reproached in this manner: "You have not wanted to do so, but waited for person-to-person supervision like an old woman would do." In the same session, fellow clients were observed using similar approaches to influence the behavior of their peers.

The visiting therapist continued his observations for several meetings of the postexercise group, and, with the consent of Mr. Casper and group members, began to assume group-member status. This enabled him to initiate change in subtle ways. The first constructive way included the increased use of "I think" and "I feel" statements rather than the accusatory "You did . . ." or "You did not . . ." statements (Froelich & Bishop, 1977). Gradually, as this interactive technique was reinforced by the visitor and then by others in the group, defensive behavior decreased. That is, as the members recognized the shift from accusation to responsibility on the part of Mr. Casper, they began to exhibit open, receptive behavior and responded to each other in ways that revealed member support as well as responsibility for their own actions. Included were positive actions toward others when in the group and the assumption of responsibilities for exercise activities outside of the group. The pseudo-stimulation of ridicule also decreased when members ceased to respond to it by nervous laughter and to begin to think of themselves as responsible enough to state in the group that admonishment was ineffective in the promotion of change.

In this illustration, it was noted that the subtle reinforcement of the visitor, the imitation of this action by Mr. Casper with reinforcement from the members, and the effects of varied verbal and nonverbal feedback within the group milieu (again, reinforcing), accomplished important group member behavior changes. Through this series of small group experiences blaming and accusatory behaviors were reduced, self-esteem was raised, communication became more constructive, and individuals assumed greater responsibilities for their own acts and for facilitating positive acts of others. Further, an improvement in the physical and general coping status of the clients was noted. The small group had accomplished a multidimensional task as adaptive coping behavior developed within each group member through a series of shared participations.

Group techniques have been learned and used effectively by counselors and other care providers. The experiential component (actual experiences within a group) plus the integration of rationale has been shown to be a productive learning method because it provides immediate feedback as members process the consequences of much of their behavior within a viable context.

RELIGION: CAUSE OR CURE?

Religion is defined as a belief in and worship of God or gods; a specific system of belief or worship, built around God, a code of ethics, or a philosophy of life (Webster, 1975). It is difficult to conceive of a person as having no religion, and yet it has been underutilized as a method of helping clients to cope. At one point in the past some student nurses were cautioned not to talk with emotionally troubled clients about sex, politics, or religion; this admonition is tantamount to instructing them to avoid being therapeutic. Surely, heinous crimes have been committed in the name of (or with the excuse of) religion from the "religious wars," the Spanish Inquisition, and witch hunts to a recently reported episode of a woman's killing herself and her five children by throwing them out of an upper-story window all because of her "religion."

These horrifying events do not obliterate the fact that some form of religious belief has been apparent in virtually every known civilization from the earliest recorded times. Glorious deeds have been religiously inspired; hospitals have been built, universities have been founded, great personal sacrifices have been made to minister to the sick, uneducated, and destitute. One could hardly read an account of experiences such as Viktor Frankl (1959) described in *Man's Search for Meaning* without deep consideration of what one's own purpose is in life. In times of illness, hospitalization of a loved one, or at any point when one is encountering a health caregiver, one may give some serious thought to what is important and what one's values really are. Is life itself of the ultimate importance or is the quality of life of equal or greater worth? These questions arise now in light of radical surgeries and life-sustaining techniques that prolong an individual's life but at great sacrifice.

Many of the models for intervention discussed in this chapter are derived from the discipline of psychology. It behooves the health caregiver to be aware that although psychologists are

> . . . supposed to exhibit empathy, acceptance and genuineness when listening to a peer discuss personal conflicts regarding anger, dependency, sex, or related issues, the quality of their behavior tends to deteriorate when listening to persons try to communicate about their conflicts in the religious or spiritual sphere. (Clement, 1978, p. 2)

Surely health care professionals have an obligation to encourage support systems that are adaptive regardless of how divergent the source might be from the one the professional might choose. While the care providers have no right to impose their religious beliefs (or sexual preferences or political leanings) on clients, they do have the obligation to support religious practices as one means of coping that has been quite effective for a number of persons for a long time.

Bell (1977) considered belief in a caring supernatural

power to be a long-term method of coping in a study she conducted to compare coping methods in mental illness and in mental wellness. Bell's data supported her hypothesis that persons exhibiting mental illness behaviors would use more short-term coping methods as compared to persons exhibiting mental wellness behaviors. Another study (McLaughlin, 1978), sought to determine the relationship between the support available to dying patients and the number of unmet needs the patients experienced. This study failed to find a relationship between religion being important to a person and that person's having fewer unmet needs than someone for whom religion was not important.

The scientific data on the effectiveness of religion as a method of coping are indeed scanty. Even more scarce, however, are studies to determine how health care providers might best utilize a client's religious orientation for the benefit of the client.

A "BRIEF THERAPY" INTERVENTION

A unique approach to problem-solving has been developed by the therapists at the Brief Therapy Center of the Mental Research Institute in Palo Alto, California (Watzlawick, Weakland, & Fisch, 1974; Weakland, Fisch, Watzlawick, & Bodin, 1974). This approach assumes that individuals are not coping adaptively with their problems of interaction with others if they come to a therapist for help implying that they are in pain or "sweating." The approach is related to learning theory in that the proponents of the approach affirm that if a difficult situation has been continuing for some time, there is something in the relationship of the patient and those with whom he or she interacts that maintains that difficult behavior. If even very minor changes in overt behavior or its verbal labeling were effected, this initial reaction may be enough to cause progressive developments (Weakland, et al., 1974).

In using brief therapy it is necessary to identify what those involved have been doing to solve the problem. The attempted solution is then identified by the therapist as the problem that he or she must work on. Sometimes the therapist exaggerates what the client is already complaining of. For example, if a client complains of being depressed, the therapist listens to the client's description of the situation, remarks that he or she really is amazed that the client is not much more depressed, and predicts that the client will, indeed, become more depressed. This prediction carries with it the implication that the client's mood can change, and if the client can get worse, it is also possible to get better.

Another example is of the mother who nagged her three teenage daughters endlessly to help more around the house. The more she nagged, the more the daughters resisted. The therapist explained that the mother was simply not nagging enough and that she should find more things to nag about and nag three times as much as she was currently doing. As a result, both the mother and the daughters grew tired of the whole scene and changed their interaction patterns so that the daughters agreed on what chores they would do and the mother gave up some of her nagging behavior.

INTERVENTION USING A COMMUNITY SUPPORT SYSTEM

Suicide or attempted suicide represents the ultimate in desperation. It is a method of coping, but it must be the most maladaptive method by any definition of maladaptiveness. In addition, when an 11-year-old child attempts suicide, it seems impossible to deny that there are flaws in that individual's support systems including the absence of opportunities to develop appropriate coping behaviors.

> Fran was 11 years old when she received her school report card on which she observed check marks indicating "needs to improve" in many areas. Subsequently, she took what was left of her mother's sleeping pills. After eight days in the City Hospital where she was admitted for the overdose, Fran was referred to the Community Mental Health Center serving the catchment area in which Fran lived.

The psychiatric-mental health nurse who followed the case made a home visit and found that Fran lived in a three-bedroom apartment in a low-cost housing development with her mother and two brothers (eight and nine years old). Fran's mother, Mrs. S., was totally blind and had a history of "nervous breakdowns" and at least one psychotic depression episode.

The following problems were identified by the family members and the nurse: Each of the children, especially Fran, wanted to spend more time with the mother. This probably reflected the mother's depressive withdrawal and lack of energy to relate actively with the children. Fran was having problems at school as were both of the boys. Mrs. S was still bathing Eric (the nine-year-old), which was of some concern to his brother, Michael, who was a year younger. The house was infested with numerous vermin (including roaches), which concerned Mrs. S and prompted her to plead with the children to confine their eating to the kitchen in order to try to control the bug problem. Most of the day Mrs. S. had nothing to do and simply sat; this information led the nurse to question whether Mrs. S's medication might need evaluating to determine if the dosage needed to be adjusted.

In addition to identifying the strengths on which to build for each of the family members, the nurse identified the support systems for this family. Individuals who were potentially supportive were identified as a cleaning lady from the Metropolitan Housing Authority, a neighbor who came in frequently to use Mrs. S's telephone and brought food, a cousin who had the family over for dinner on occasion, and the teacher with whom Fran felt comfortable. The agencies, in addition to the City Hospital and Mental Health Center already mentioned, included Adult Family Services, the Department of Family and Children Services, Agency for the Blind, Vocational Rehabilitation Services, Big Brother Services, the elementary school where all of the children attended classes, and the insect exterminating company.

After eight weeks of working with this family and coordinating all of the support systems, the nurse indicated that definite gains had been made. The family members were spending more time with each other and had plans to attend school functions together. Mrs. S. had completed the initial procedures necessary for personal and vocational training by working with the representative from Vocational Rehabilitation in his assessment of her skills in reading Braille. She had obtained the initial material for preparing for a proofreading job that she could do in her home and earn up to nine dollars per hour. Mrs. S. had contracted with the exterminators for monthly services, and the children were cooperating by eating in the kitchen exclusively. Mrs. S's medication was discontinued and the entire family seemed to be happier and excited about Mrs. S's new career goals.

COUNTERCONDITIONING AS SOCIAL LEARNING THEORY APPLICATION

The social learning theorists have influenced a range of care providers to examine methods of behavior change that are not greatly dependent upon the identification and/or understanding of the historical antecedents of the maladaptive and asocial behavior. In other words, behavioral conditioning can be accomplished primarily through an emphasis on the particular maladaptive behavior the client exhibits instead of how he or she developed that behavior. Mowrer (1960) examined the classical conditioning studies and postulated that the salivary or muscle responses of the animal were only partial reactions of the complex emotional pattern initiated when the bell signaled food. He explained that the dog "felt good" or "hopeful" with the signal and that the salivary or muscle response was a companion of this emotional reaction in the stimulus circumstance. Further, the converse of hope, fear, developed when the conditioning stimulus was accompanied by discomfort. In summary, Mowrer stated that this conditioning was more complex than the early classical conditioning paradigm in that the learned responses were emotional responses to stimuli—primarily in the general categories of hope and fear. Bugelski (1964) extended the premise through his contention that almost all learned sets of behavior consisted of the performance of those responses the individual was already able to perform. Ultimately, then, hope and fear became important components of performance behavior because these conditioned emotions were powerful directives for other responses.

As a consequence of this thesis, emphasis moved to the application of the principles of counterconditioning by some caregivers in the modification of the emotional component, thereby influencing the overall performance of the client. To summarize, the learned behavior of a client included an emotional response. If that response prevented development of healthy coping responses and subsequent adaptive performance patterns, it tended to keep the client unhealthy. If, for example, a client could not use the elevators needed in tall buildings, because of a fear of elevators, closed spaces, heights, or all three, this required that the client always walk to upper floors or remain on lower floors. The desired new learning was not restricted to learning to ride the elevator—in itself a rather simple feat—but extended to counterconditioning the accompanying fear or anxiety, which was a learned response paired with riding elevators, being in closed spaces, heights, or all three.

With the elimination of the fear, according to the theory, a hopeful response will be acquired by the individual and the range of prosocial and adaptive behavior increased. Subsequently, the newly acquired behavior may increase the options of the client in many facets of life, including living arrangements, occupational choices, employment selection, and leisure time activities.

COUNTERCONDITIONING: RECIPROCAL INHIBITION THROUGH SYSTEMATIC DESENSITIZATION

The systematic use of desensitization as counterconditioning to reduce fear, anxiety, and avoidance behavior has been tested extensively in the past two decades (Wolpe, 1954; 1969). However, as early as 1924 (Jones, 1924), a desensitization-type procedure was used to modify the fearfulness of furry white animals and other similar objects in a child. Since this technique was the reversal of an earlier fear-producing conditioning procedure of Watson and Rayner (1920), it was described as counterconditioning.

In the classical desensitization program the individual is exposed to graduated procedures in order to modify (desensitize) the learned maladaptive behavior bit by bit. However, this does not preclude the possibility of the "one-dose" desensitization, that is, a client may be able to desensitize his or her learned maladaptive behavior as a whole.

Theorists and therapists as cited earlier have disagreed

concerning the processes of desensitization as well as the protocol for the use of desensitization. In the early development of desensitization, Wolpe (1954) and his colleagues subscribed to a systematic approach in which clients used reciprocal inhibition as counterconditioning. The Wolpe paradigm relied upon the presentation, in imagery or reality, of the fear- or anxiety-provoking situation, or any part of it that was the primary cause of the maladaptive response, together with a form of counterconditioning, that is, Jacobson's relaxation (1938). The relaxation acted as an inhibitory process through the autonomic nervous system. This paradigm, referred to in Chapter 2, was based on the premise that sympathetic and parasympathetic responsiveness tended to be physiologically antagonistic. He assumed that muscular relaxation and certain other pleasurable stimulations elicited parasympathetic responses that inhibited the dominant sympathetic anxiety responses (the maladaptive behavior). This peripheral theory of anxiety was questioned (Bandura, 1969; Davison & Valins, 1968) because some research indicated that autonomic and avoidance responses were not essentially causally linked but were coeffects that operated subcortically, as in the reticular activating system, instead of in the autonomic nervous system.

Other findings or positions have been provocative. Animal experimentation demonstrated that the removal of peripheral autonomic responses only affected partially the acquisition of avoidance behavior. Rescorla and Solomon (1967) proposed that instrumental responsiveness was regulated mainly by central mediators, ones that could be established and/or eliminated through the procedures of classical conditioning. Lomont (1965) proposed that extinction was the mechanism of change, as opposed to the Wolpe theory of reciprocal inhibition. Valins and Ray (1967) and Davison (1966) contended that cognitive and expectational influences were strong variables in the changed behavior. Rimm and Medieros (1970), Davison (1965), Wolpin and Rainer (1966), and Cooke (1968) observed that desensitization was possible without the relaxation component.

Since the Wolpe model and its variations have been tested

for a long period of time with some acclaim, this model is summarized here. Initially, three stages of operations were identified in the procedure. Each required the collaboration of the client and therapist. In the first stage, deep muscle relaxation was mastered by the client through a series of training and practice sessions. The second stage consisted of client-constructed personal anxiety or fear hierarchies needed for the third stage, in which the treatment itself was presented. This treatment consisted of the institution of the relaxation sequence by the client counterposed with the anxiety- or fear-provoking stimuli from the hierarchies. The treatment period for each session ended at a point determined by mutual client- and therapist-derived goals for therapy, but primarily influenced by the client's response to controlled exposure to gradations of provocative stimuli. That is, the client acknowledged that he or she had achieved a state of fearlessness or relative comfortableness to a set of stimuli during a particular time period (experienced desensitization) but was not ready to proceed to other, more intense stimuli of the hierarchy in that session. Following a designated hierarchy presentation, the relaxation exercise was repeated in the Wolpe protocol in order to eliminate any residual fear or discomfort that may continue to develop prior to the succeeding session(s) (Wolpe & Lazarus, 1966).

This protocol, with successively designated gradations of stimuli from the hierarchies, was continued for several sessions until the treatment of the client appeared effective. At the conclusion of the designed sessions, treatment effectiveness was validated by several methods, including the use of pre- and posttests, self-report, psychological and physiological evaluations, and through the examination of client behavior in actual experiential situations.

In conclusion, according to the theory, a successful treatment series using desensitization for behavior change in a client will be one in which maladaptive responses are inhibited in order for the client to be free to show latent adaptive behavior and/or to learn new adaptive ways of coping.

COUNTERCONDITIONING: VICARIOUS CONDITIONING AND EXTINCTION THROUGH MODELING

Another counterconditioning application uses vicarious conditioning and extinction through modeling (Bandura & Walters, 1963; Bugelski, 1964; and Mowrer, 1960). Through this process, clients with restrictive learned fear, anxiety, or avoidance behaviors that impede prosocial or adaptive performance are able to observe models reacting to events in the environment. This observation makes it possible for the observer to avoid directly any uncomfortable or previously learned consequences as well as to observe the effects of the actions on the model. Theoretically, through this experience the undesired set of responses, such as fearfulness, that would increase anxiety and avoidance in the observer can be extinguished in the modeling process because the observer avoids the direct consequences of the act and their reinforcing properties. An application of vicarious conditioning follows.

> For a variety of reasons Ms. SN showed avoidance behavior toward any clients with tracheostomies. One fear may have been that the clients would lack proper airway care and suffer dire consequences from the lack of oxygen. When the instructor of this student nurse noted this pattern of behavior she arranged for an expert nurse to model appropriate behavior with this kind of client in order for Ms. SN to observe in the modeling condition. During the modeling event the model, Mr. A., performed each element of the interaction and the basic procedure of tracheostomy care without any expectation for action by the student other than observation. This included no direct acceptance of the consequences of the actions by the student. The student, then, observed the performance of the model but did not have to experience the consequences of the performance or their reinforcing properties. Indeed, the student as observer noted that the client responded well to the treatment with evidence of a clear airway, natural-appearing skin tone, decreased restlessness, and an overall expression of comfort. The model, Mr. A., relaxed his stance of readiness displayed during the procedure, gave the client positive feedback in the form of a pat on the shoulder and an encouraging statement, and made the client's situation as stress-free as possible under the circumstances. As the observer, Ms. SN, emotionally re-

corded these consequences, and according to the theory, her fearfulness was reduced and the next set of behaviors from the hierarchy
of responses was enabled to emerge.

In summary, the next set of responses in the hierarchy will
probably not be maladaptive or uncomfortable as was the fearfulness, but may be adaptive and healthy. With extinction or
reduction of the maladaptive response, the individual may be
freed to use other, previously-acquired behaviors to accomplish
the expected objectives (as the performance of the tracheostomy
care for the client), thus moving to the healthy end of the
behavior continuum. If, however, the next set of behaviors is
maladaptive, the use of other systematic procedures may shape
the desired behavior and direct the energy of the individual
toward the development of prosocial means of gratification.

As stated in Chapter 2, Bandura and Walters summarized
the three possible effects of exposure to a model for imitative
purposes as the modeling effect, an inhibitory effect, and a
possible eliciting effect. When the imitative responses are re-
produced in the client's performance, the pattern of consequences to him or her largely determines whether these will be
strengthened, weakened, or inhibited, according to the theory
of reinforcement (Bandura & Walters, 1963). Further, Mowrer
(1960) and Bugelski (1964) emphasized that the changed behavior of the client is primarily the consequence of emotional
counterconditioning.

Mowrer (1960) distinguished between two forms of imitative learning in terms of reinforcement. In one form, the
model performs and rewards the observer simultaneously.
Through repetitions, the observer gradually acquires the response repertory. In the other form, the model exhibits the
responses and experiences the consequences and reinforcement. This enables the observer to experience empathetically
the total effect of the behavior of the model, thereby acquiring
greater gains through this higher order of vicarious conditioning. In summary, the client (as observer) learns through his or
her observation of the reinforcement of the behavior of another, a model, and from the feedback which serves as rein-

forcement for the conditioning or extinction of his or her own particular behavior.

As a result of the modeling experience, clients have learned intricate performance patterns, conditioned emotional responses, vicariously extinguished fearful and avoidant behavior without adverse consequences to themselves, induced inhibitions through witnessing punishment to others, and enhanced and socially regulated expressions of influential models (Bandura, 1969).

Summary of the Modeling Process

The modeling process has been summarized by Bandura (1969). Initially, the response in the client occurs through covert symbolic processes during the period of exposure to the modeling stimuli and prior to the overt response or to the appearance of the reinforcing events. Apparently, observational learning entails symbolic coding, with the organization of modeling stimuli represented in memory. Subsequently, these symbolic forms are transformed to motor equivalents. The matching responses result primarily from stimulus contiguity and associated symbolic processes. The reinforcement acts collaboratively (after Skinner) following a few exposures, by the promotion of vigilance (attentiveness to cues) in clients of modeling behavior. Further, "vigilance behavior" itself has been increased in clients through a series of measures that promote their attentiveness to what was present, who was present, and the content of the messages (verbal and nonverbal) in given situations.

The examination of a series of investigations in which modeling was used to modify client behavior indicated that vicarious means of presentation (through the use of films, tapes, imagery, or slides showing a model's behavior) as well as live modeling methods were effective (Bandura, 1962, 1969; Bandura & Kupers, 1974; Bandura & Menlove, 1968; Davis, McLemore, & London, 1970; Kazdin, 1979; Lang, Melamed, & Hart, 1970). The ultimate assessment of the changed behavior, however, has been in terms of the posttests, those tests that use actual situational or experiential performance to indicate whether or not the client did, in fact, change his or her behavior and whether or not that behavior was maintained over a period of time. Additional examples further depict and contrast the use of these two modalities as tested interventions.

Desensitization

A client-therapist situation in which the desensitization of an overtly evident fear held by a new mother for her malformed infant illustrates an application of reciprocal inhibition as counterconditioning.

The mother may be disappointed in her ability to produce a normal infant as well as in her ability to offer care to her offspring. She may turn away physically and emotionally in her fear and avoidance of what she perceives as a potentially threatening situation. Her behavior may include grief manifestations, expressions of discomfort, symptoms of illness, or feigned displays of acceptance. Each behavior should be identified in order to provide the caregiver with an assessment of the baseline behavior and a basis for planning the intervention. If desensitization is the method of choice predicted to overcome the avoidance and fearful behavior of the mother toward her infant, one of several forms may be useful.

The most frequently tested forms of desensitization are protocols that modify a series of gradations of fearful behavior until the desired behavior is obtained and protocols that expose the client to the "full blown" end situation (implosion or "flooding"). The latter may be accomplished through imagery or a simulation of actuality (Stampfl & Levis, 1967).

In the gradual approach, the client and care provider construct a hierarchy consisting of least to most uncomfortable (anxiety- and fear-provoking) situations perceived in the total behavior. For the mother in the example, the hierarchy may range from being in the home with the infant to the actual physical attention and emotional mothering responses. The treatment may require that the mother as client master relaxation techniques to be used before and after each encounter session with the stimuli of the hierarchy and become comfortable with each stimulus before moving up the hierarchy to the more intense stimuli. The hierarchy may be given to the client as imagery, as a videotaped encounter, or through the *in vivo* situation.

The proponents of the bit-by-bit protocol prefer to desensitize the behavior in an orderly manner, whereas the therapists who use implosion plunge the client into the most anxiety- and fear-provoking situation the client can imagine in order to expend the maximum energy and reveal the consequences of that exposure immediately. In the aforementioned mother-infant situation, implosion for the mother may require her to imagine the most feared and anxiety-provoking interaction involved in caring for her child. She would be encouraged to hold this image intensely, to feel it overwhelm her. Or, she may view slides or view live mother-child interactions that intensely depict her fears and discomfort. As an outcome of this intensity the mother, with the help of the therapist, may realize that she is able to cope, that the situation is one that is very difficult but that she can learn to deal with, given time and assistance.

The treatment with desensitization as presented above is considered adequate or complete when the client is able to demonstrate that she can perform the desired behavior without undue discomfort or fear. In addition to the actual demonstration (the changed behavior), the caregiver may wish to contrast a variety of measurements from pre- to postintervention. For example, the physiological measurements of blood pressure and pulse rate, the self-report, and the observations of approach behavior and the participation in actual caregiving in particular situations may be considered as indices in the evaluation of pre- to postintervention levels of behavior in clients. Whereas the physiological mechanisms can be controlled in many individuals through learning, these autonomic responses are more difficult for many clients to master unintentionally; hence, they are considered to be valid indicators when combined with other methods to assess behavioral responses. This form of assessment can also be used to evaluate the effectivenss of other counterconditioning methods.

Modeling

If modeling is used as a form of vicarious extinction in the modification of the behavior of the mother in the example, the mother may be exposed to live models giving care to her infant or to one with a similar problem. The modeling also is effective if videotapes are used as demonstration (Bandura & Menlove, 1968). Recall that the client is exposed to the potentially threatening modeling cues without the real threat of the consequences, that is, her malformed infant is given loving, safe care (a feeding, for example) by a model-as-mother who performs the physical and mothering component of the care in a loving, warm manner and is not overwhelmed or "harmed" by the experience. Through a series of episodes (modeling encounters), each demonstrating to the observer that the model interacts humanely and appropriately in the situation(s) feared and/ or avoided by the client, the client not only evades the perceived threat but sees that the elements of the demonstrated behavior may become her own desired mothering behavior.

For example, the mother may perceive that she has nothing to fear from caring for her infant, that her infant needs almost the identical care that she learned prenatally to give to any normal infant. And without the fearfulness of the consequences (e.g., that she may harm the infant or that it may be harmful to her to give care to the child) she can learn to provide the requisite care. In fact, according to the theory, she already has the skills and can perform them once the fearfulness has been reduced or extinguished.

In summary, through the modeling approach, realism is presented to the client, that is, the model may demonstrate her own coping powers as she progresses to the desired behavior and its consequences. Kazdin (1973) noted that the coping influence of a model affected treatment outcomes in clients in a positive direction. Therefore, modeling in which the development of coping behavior is demonstrated appears to increase the effectiveness of the client outcomes.

The examples presented here indicated that clients were able to reduce the maladaptive pseudoneurotic fear and anxiety learned earlier and consequently perform the desired adaptive behavior without the use of lengthy, expensive psychoanalytic treatment modalities. Further, many elements of the desired behavior probably were present in the repertory of the client; therefore, these elements emerged readily in the formation of new patterns of responses upon the elimination of the previously learned restrictive fearfulness and its accompanying discomfort.

COUNTERCONDITIONING:
RELAXATION TECHNIQUES

In the past, care providers often sought to relieve the tension of their clients with the suggestion that they relax. The effectiveness of this was difficult to assess because of the many physiological and psychological variables involved. However, Jacobson (1938) presented evidence that muscle relaxation and certain other pleasurable stimulations elicited parasympathetic responses that inhibited dominant sympathetic anxiety responses. Hess (1957), also demonstrated in his investigations of responses of the hypothalamus that adynomia of the skeletal musculature decreased blood pressure and respiratory rate. Since 1958, Wolpe, as noted in the previous section, has tested these findings repeatedly as he and his colleagues have used relaxation techniques in desensitization protocols. Although some of the later study findings have shown that the use of relaxation is not essential for the accomplishment of desensitization (Lang & Lazovik, 1963; Lang, Lazovik, & Reynolds, 1965; Lang, 1964), other studies have indicated that relaxation is more effective than the "no treatment" category in behavior modification research (Davison, 1965; Green, Webster, Beiman, Rosmarin, & Holliday, 1981; Rachman, 1965). Recently, care providers have sought a nonpharmacological mechanism to relieve tension; therefore, the practice of autogenic techniques in the form of systematic relaxation has emerged as an alternative to medication in the management of the stressors of anxiety and some kinds of pain in particular clients (Benson

& Goodale, 1981; Budzynski, Stoyva, & Adler, 1973; Hess, 1957).

The benefits of the use of systematic relaxation techniques are documented in the research of Green, et al., 1981. Moreover, the care provider may offer relaxation protocols in various ways. The initial instructions may be given individually or in groups, in written or verbal form (including the use of audio or audiovisual tapes). Further, the use of biofeedback, through which the client monitors the outcomes of his efforts, increases the effectiveness of the technique (Haynes, et al., 1975, Kinsman, et al., 1975). Clients may be selective as to the time of use and individualize the focus on the musculature and mood state according to the perceived need. Finally, this is an economical form of treatment that ultimately promotes client independence because of the nature of the administration. However, as with other forms of self care, the relaxation protocol should be monitored by the care provider through observation of the client at intervals in order to facilitate the use of "good form," note progress, and review the general welfare of the client to ensure that any new developments are recognized. This observation would include screening for new reasons for anxiety or pain that may require additional assessment and other therapy.

Instructions for the adaptation of the often-used Wolpe Relaxation Technique are as follows:[1]

> Relaxation of the upper body can be obtained by getting as comfortable as possible. Relax on a bed or lean back in a comfortable chair. As you relax, clinch your right fist; clinch it tighter and tighter. Feel the tension as you do so. Keep it tight and feel the tension in your right fist, hand, forearm. Now relax. Let the fingers of your right hand become loose, and note the contrast in the feeling. Now let yourself go, and try to relax all over.
>
> Again, clinch your right fist, tight, hold it, and notice the tense feeling again. Now, let go; extend your fingers straight out. Note the difference again. Repeat this with your left fist. Make your left fist tight while you relax the rest of your body. Clinch it tighter; feel the tension; now, relax. Notice and enjoy the relaxed feeling. Repeat again;

[1]Adapted from Wolpe, J., & Lazarus, A. *Behavior therapy techniques: Guide to the treatment of neurosis.* Copyright © 1966 by Pergamon Press, London, England. Used with permission.

clinch, then relax. Continue for awhile. Do this with your forearms. Notice the sensations. Continue with your hands, forearms, then bend your arms to tense the biceps. Tense them harder. Observe the tense feeling. Straighten out your arms, relax, and feel the difference. Let relaxation develop. Again, tense, hold it, then relax. Each time pay close attention to the sensation of tension and relaxation. Now, straighten your arms; straighten so that you feel the most tension in the triceps along the back of your arms. Stretch your arms and notice the tension. Now, relax; place your arms in a comfortable position. Let the relaxation proceed on its own. Notice how heavy and comfortable your arms feel as you let them relax. Straighten the arms once more in order to feel the tension in the triceps muscles. Feel the tension and relax. Let your arms be as comfortable as possible; let them relax more and more. Continue to relax. Even when they feel relaxed, try to move to deeper and deeper levels of relaxation.

For relaxation of the facial area, neck, shoulders, and upper back, let all of your muscles go loose and heavy. Just settle back quietly and comfortably. Wrinkle your forehead, relax, and smooth it out. Picture your entire forehead and scalp becoming smoother and smoother as the relaxation continues. Now, frown and crease your brows and notice the tension. Let go of the tension again; smooth out the forehead once more. Now, close your eyes, tighter and tighter, feel the tension. Relax your eyes. Keep your eyes closed, comfortable, and notice the relaxation. Now clench your jaws and bite your teeth together. Notice the tension throughout your jaws. Now, relax your jaws, and part your lips slightly. Notice the relaxation. Press your tongue hard against the roof of your mouth. Feel the tension; then let your tongue return to a comfortable and relaxed position. Now, purse your lips and press them together, tighter and tighter. Relax them, and notice the contrast between tension and relaxation. Feel the relaxation all over your face, your forehead, scalp, eyes, jaws, lips, tongue, and throat. The relaxation progresses further and further. Now work with your neck muscles; press your head back as far as possible, and feel the tension in your neck. Roll it to the right and feel the tension shift. Now roll it to the left.

Straighten your neck; bring your head forward, and press your chin against your chest. Return your head to a comfortable position, and notice the relaxation. Let it develop. Shrug your shoulders up and hold the tension in this position. Drop the shoulders and feel the relaxation.

The neck and shoulders are relaxed. Shrug your shoulders and move them around; bring them up, forward, back. Drop them again, and relax. Let the relaxation spread deep into your shoulders and your back muscles; relax your neck and throat, jaws, facial areas, and let relaxation take over and grow deeper and deeper.

To relax your chest, abdomen, and lower back, loosen your whole body completely. Feel how heavy and comfortable your body becomes. Breathe easily in and out. Notice the increased relaxation with exhalation; just breathe out and relax. Now, breathe in and fill your lungs. Inhale deeply and hold your breath. Notice the tension. Now, exhale, letting the chest walls become loose, and push out the air automatically. Continue to relax and breathe freely and easily. Feel the relaxation. While relaxed, fill your lungs again; breathe deeply and hold it. Now breathe out and notice the relief. Breathe normally. Continue to relax and let relaxation spread to your back, shoulders, neck, arms. Let go, and enjoy the relaxation. Now, pay attention to the abdominal muscles. Tighten the muscles of your abdomen and make it hard. Notice the tension. Relax, and let the muscles loosen; note the contrast. When relaxed, notice the well-being from the relaxation of your abdomen. Now pull your abdominal muscles in; let the muscles become tight; feel the tension; then relax the muscles. Continue to breathe normally and feel the gentle massaging action throughout your chest and abdomen. Now, pull the abdomen in and hold it. Feel the tension; then relax fully. Let the tension dissolve as the relaxation grows deeper. Each time you breathe out, observe the rhythmic relaxation in your lungs and abdomen. Notice how relaxation increases. Try to let go all the contractions in your body. Now direct your attention to your lower back; make it hollow, and feel the tension along your spine; then settle back and be comfortable, and relax the lower back. Now arch up your back and notice the tension as you do so. Keep the rest of your body as relaxed as possible. Try to keep the tension localized throughout your lower back. Relax once again, more and more. Relax the lower back, upper back, your abdomen, chest, shoulders, arms, facial area; relax more and more, deeper.

To relax your hips, thighs, calves, and then your complete body, just let go of all your tensions. Now, flex your buttocks and thighs. Flex your thighs by pressing down your heels as hard as you can. Relax and notice the difference. Straighten your knees and flex your thigh muscles again. Hold the tension. Relax your hips and thighs and let the relaxation move on its own. Press your feet and toes downward, away from your face in order to tense your calf muscles. Note the tension. Relax your calves and feet. Now, bend your feet toward your face and feel the tension along your shins. Bring your toes up. Relax again. Try relaxing awhile. Now let yourself relax deeper and deeper. Relax your feet, ankles, calves, shins, knees, thighs, buttocks, and hips. Notice the feeling of heaviness in your lower body. Now spread the relaxation to your abdomen, waist, lower back; just let go. Feel how relaxed you can become. Let this relaxation spread to your upper back, chest, shoulders, arms, and to the finger tips. Relax more and more. Just let go and let no tension creep into your throat; relax your neck, jaws, and your facial muscles. Keep relaxing your whole body like that for a while. Just let yourself relax.

Now you can become twice as relaxed as you are by taking a deep breath and slowly exhaling. Close your eyes so that you are less aware of the objects and movements around you. This prevents surface tensions from developing. Breathe in deeply and feel yourself becoming heavier and heavier. Inhale deeply and exhale very slowly. Notice how heavy and relaxed you have become.

In perfect relaxation states you won't feel like moving a single muscle of your body. Think about the effort of raising your right arm. As you think of this, see if any tensions have crept into your shoulder and arm. Now, decide not to lift your arm, but to continue relaxation. Notice the relief and disappearance of the tension.

Practice this relaxation for a few minutes. When you wish to get up, count backwards from four to one. You should feel fine and refreshed, wide awake and calm.

Whereas the Wolpe Technique requires a rather precise training and practicing protocol, stimulus words may be used to initiate and induce relaxation in clients. For example, a particular stimulus phrase such as a word or phrase that expresses a favorite restful state may be paired with relaxation until the expression of the term itself induces the relaxed state. This form of counterconditioning may be so conditioned that the client may become able to use it "on the spot" in almost any circumstance. Benson and Goodale identified the requisites for self-induced relaxation as a quiet environment, decreased muscle tonus, a mental device, and a passive attitude (1981, p 266). The following situation demonstrates an application of this method.

> Mr. Selby was a "driver." He probably "drove" himself more relentlessly and constantly than he drove others in his small successful hardware enterprise. However, as his business thrived, his health appeared threatened and he noted greater difficulty with sleep, digestive processes, and interpersonal relationships. It was increasingly difficult for him to change his tempo after meetings, sales ventures, or the usual business or family relationships in which decisions were made. One of the suggestions given to him during a health status evaluation was his need to relax, to pause periodically or as he sensed the need to reduce his mounting tension and to use a mental device in the form of a stimulus word such as "slow" as he initiated relaxation.
>
> In spite of Mr. Selby's insistence that the need for relaxation was not his problem, he was finally convinced that he should try to break away voluntarily from activities that increased muscle and psychic tension. He agreed to learn to use the referred-to process through which a stimulus word initiated relaxation, thereby finding that a method under his control was very satisfactory. He reported to his physician that the method was more effective than the use of medications because of the lack of side effects. Also, this program was economical!

While the application of counterconditioning by nurses and other caregivers requires the mastery of special skills derived from particular learning theories and innovative adaptations, the results of these interventions have been encouraging thus far.

INTERVENTION USING GAME
THEORY APPLICATION

Application of the techniques from game theory has been successfully used to modify social behavior as well as to entertain. Although this theory initially was grounded in a sociological context, mathematicians related mathematics to social situations in which players were permitted to test and modify their strategies in terms of a "payoff" model. The payoff model offered incentives for risk taking, problem solving, and creativity. Owen (1968) identified the three elements of the game as the *alternative moves* (by personal or random chance), the *possible lack of knowledge*, and the *payoff function*.

The first two elements enable players to make decisions and risk moves; test the effectiveness of their moves in contrast to their other options or to the moves of other players; and develop strategies that increase their knowledge and enhance their problem-solving abilities. The payoff element gives information for adequacy or inadequacy, that is, the players receive feedback relative to the effectiveness of their moves or choices in the game in comparison to their terminal positions. Also this payoff provides the stimulation and incentive that maintain the interest of the players over a period of time. In a successful game, or series of game interactions, the theory implies that forms of repeated reinforcement for the positive choices as part of the feedback will have the strength to alter future client behavior in the game category. The insight, knowledge, and skills gained through the game exercise will probably be tested by the client and become part of that individual's coping behavior.

To demonstrate the application of the above, the reader can examine a situation facing a growing number of career women in Western culture today; that is, the delayed childbearing period versus the option of bearing no children. Among the choices that the family planning counselor or nurse has to offer a client with this dilemma is the use of a game in which the individual may be exposed to the options of a child or childless family, make choices, and test these in terms of the expected immediate and long range outcomes.

The game designed for this situation may offer several players with the same dilemma opportunities to explore the simulated effects of several lifestyles (child versus childless) on the women and their spouses. Included would be the responsibilities and attitudes relative to caring for an unhealthy child (because of the heightened risk factor in the older mother); the older primipara and parenting family; and socioeconomic considerations. The explorations may extend beyond the effects of the above on the nuclear family and include the impact on close relatives, significant others, and the communities for living and working.

Inherent in this game, then, may be a range of biosociocultural considerations, many of which are most difficult to verbalize and to problem-solve hypothetically. In fact, when the confrontation is made, the difficult areas usually overwhelm the individual, thereby overriding the balances that should be recognized. For example, the woman may dwell on the possibility of the unhealthy child. The advantage of the game context, hence, may be in the exposure of players to a balance of alternative situations. Further, in the game the client is enabled to think and respond in ways that may allow the nurse or counselor and the client to reinforce ideas and strategies that enhance positive coping behavior.

Duke (1974) preferred a game simulation in which a conceptual map developed by the players conveys information about the problem to be solved or the communication to be achieved. That is, again, the game to be developed reflects some complex reality or a substitute for it. An example would be the simulation of a reality situation in which the players depict their strategies for coping with a crisis, such as, a group of adolescents dealing with separation from familiar surroundings wherein the youth needed 24 hours a day of extended care in a rehabilitation center (McDowell, Coven, & Eash, 1979).

The leader or counselor of such a group would not have all of the desired strategies in mind but would identify the problem or assist the group members as players to distinguish the problem to be solved from all possible problems.

> One small group of clients identified its emerging problem as the increased invasion of privacy by care providers in the new rehabilitative setting. The group identified this as the most salient problem

of all of the problems because of the group's assistance in the maintenance of body functions, hygiene, and status. All of the problems were, however, personal and important because of the individual biopsychosocial stages of development. The group members communicated their perceptions about the problem and worked through a strategy that was successful, thereby enhancing morale and furthering the accomplishment of therapy goals.

This exercise began with the verbal expressions of the thoughts and feelings of the group members. As the members expressed themselves, they eventually agreed on the important ideas that should be written as notes about the invasion of privacy. A medium-sized flipchart was used because it could be assembled readily, the notes were easy to write and read at almost eye level, and the pages of the chart were handy for the participants to use as they referred to ideas stated earlier in the deliberations. One member was selected to record the ideas expressed. He wrote key words or phrases that captured the ideas, using a large script to facilitate reading.

As the discussion of the ideas continued, the subsequent pages of the flipchart became more formalized, and arrows were included to show the members the direction of the ideas or step sequences as indicated. For example, a notation may have stated that "First, we must do this. . . . " Eventually, the leader was able to assist the members in the formulation of a simple statement of their problem within the context of a realistic solution. With the additional examination of the words and phrases on the flipchart by the members, the leader was enabled to identify themes that dealt with the overall problem of invasion of privacy. The themes included various meanings of the problem for the members, for example, the fear of intrusion by care providers when engaged in actions considered private, such as toileting, which was complicated by the fact that the personal limitations imposed by physical conditions required the assistance of care providers. Further, the members were able to state that these intrusions were not only embarrassing, but increased feelings of low self-esteem and status, of particular importance during the developmental stage of youth wherein independence was valued highly but physical dependence was an unexpected outcome of certain handicapping conditions.

As the group members pursued their discussions of the theme content, they were enabled by the feedback of the leader and each other to identify objectives that were achievable and would possibly assist in the maintenance of elements of privacy through acceptable methods. Also, the objectives that demonstrated the desires of the members to increase the power and control over their own welfare were predicted to enhance the morale of the group, alter some of the responsibilities of the caregivers, and probably create disequilibrium between caregivers and the recipients of their care until a satisfactory state of collaboration developed.

Finally, methods for the achievement of the objectives were formulated. These methods included tasks to be performed by the group members and those to be delegated to caregivers (including family members of the clients). The development of this set of procedures to accomplish a purpose tested the application of game theory in that all members of the group were permitted to express their ideas; visualize how realistic the ideas were when examined by other members in terms of the payoff as benefits; compromise; again examine the payoff; and reach consensus about courses of action and ways to implement the actions and assess their effectiveness. As the members of the group participated in the process, they actually formulated a conceptual map in which ideas were captured from brainstorming about the dilemma; themes from this collection of ideas were identified; the problem was clarified; objectives for action and methods for accomplishment were identified; and the eventual institution of a plan to resolve the problem emerged. Ultimately, the members would be enabled to participate in an evaluation by the game method in order to assess overall effectiveness of the game activity as well as the changes produced in the lives of the members such as the consequence of revisions in client care by the system.

EXERCISE AS A THERAPEUTIC ALTERNATIVE

Exercise, whether it is called physical therapy, slimnastics, recreation, or physical education, is widely recognized for its health-enhancing benefits. Colleges and universities, for example, have been requiring a minimum number of credits to be earned in physical education for a number of years. More recently, hospitals and clinics have instituted exercise programs for patients with cardiac and other physical problems. Until quite recently, the "in" thing for women to wear to the grocery store was the tennis dress, but the popularity of this outfit is being eclipsed by jogging shorts.

In addition to the obvious physical benefits of exercise including weight control, muscle toning, endurance building, and skill learning, there are many claims being made about the psychological benefits of exercise. The ultimate goal of Judo, for example, is to train a sound mind while developing a harmonious body. "Judo may appear purely physical on the surface, but its true nature is the fulfillment of both physical and mental health" (Fukuda, 1973). The most widely accepted claims, however, seem to be those made about running.

In San Francisco, in 1978, some 16,000 people ran 7.6 miles in what is called the Bay to Creakers Race. That same year, on the other side of the country, more than 12,000 individuals ran 6.2 miles in the Peachtree Road Race in Atlanta and more than 4,000 ran the 26 miles of the Boston Marathon. Every weekend local races occur all over the country, and many newspaper columns, sports sections, popular magazines, and professional journals have been devoted to trying to explain such behavior. Dr. Ray Foley, chairperson of the psychology department at the University of Alabama and a runner himself, is quoted as saying:

> The average adult in this day and age in a normal day has between five and ten things weighing on his mind. There are bills to pay, articles to write, relationships to worry about, job responsibilities, and a million other things. Some people even worry about things during their sleeping hours. But when your mind begins to enter into its relaxed state, it's almost impossible to concentrate on any one thing; much less five or ten things. Running relieves these pressures much the same way a martini or Valium would; only without the harmful effects. (Foley, 1978)

Several physicians who are runners have written about the positive effects of running. Ullyot (1976) wrote that running "is not 'exercise.' This is living to one's fullest capacity. All the health benefits of exercise are peripheral to this euphoria. They do come, but just as gravy to add on the main dish" (p.4). Sheehan (1975), a cardiac specialist, described himself as a mainline jogger who gets withdrawal symptoms if he goes for more than 48 hours without running. Sheehan believes that running will bring to one those values sought by all: "the habit of contemplation developed in solitary long runs, the art of conversation found again in running with a companion, the sense of community born in the communal anticipation, agony and eventual relaxation of the competitive race, and finally the development of maximum physical capabilities which in turn help us to find one maximum spiritual and intellectual potential" (p. 30). Glasser (1976) described running as a "positive addiction" because individuals who run experience "withdrawal symptoms," as noted by Sheehan, if they do not run.

Running as therapy was described by Kostrubala (1976), who ran with a group of his patients. They ran for an hour and met as a group for a second hour. Kostrubala believes that running is a potentially effective method of treating such problems as depression, schizophrenia, anorexia nervosa, obesity, alcoholism, and excessive smoking. He pointed out that there has never been a proven death from coronary disease in anyone who has finished a marathon (a 26-mile race) within seven years after finishing.

> Sylvia was a 20-year-old college student who was worried about everything. She expressed concern about her grades, her social life was particularly anxiety-provoking, and she had difficulty sleeping and eating. Her nurse-therapist suggested that she run around the track three or four times per day to work off some of the "nervousness" she was experiencing. The exercise proved to be much more beneficial for Sylvia, who could eat and sleep appropriately after jogging, than the medications that had been previously prescribed by her family physician.

Other health caregivers will be of more help to their clients if they remember that exercise, too, can be an alternative to medication and other forms of therapy.

Caution, common sense, and professional responsibility are obviously indicated in the use of exercise. All activity should be evaluated with regard to the potential impact, positive and negative, on the client.

CONCLUSION

The summaries presented of the intervention modalities and the accompanying examples of their uses with clients who show maladaptive coping behaviors have been selected because these techniques for the development of adaptive coping can be learned and applied in a variety of settings. The selection included some forms of treatment that require intensive study and supervised practice, whereas others may be existing but untested components of the care provider's armamentarium.

The primary criterion in the judgment of ethical implications for all forms of social influence, according to Kelman (1965; 1972) is the degree to which freedom of choice is protected in an individual. Bandura (1969) added that the "sense of obligation" as a therapist characteristic is important, whereas Rokeach and Regan (1980) reminded us of the function of values in counseling, or in any care providing situation. It is hoped that the foregoing discussions of a variety of ways to be assistive to clients with coping problems has widened the options of choices for care providers in the services they give individuals who need help in particular life situations.

Chapter 5

Implications for Consultation, Education, and Research

In the previous four chapters coping and related terms have been defined from a psychological as well as a physiological point of view; cases have been presented and the healthy and unhealthy coping behaviors of each have been identified; and models for intervention have been presented. There is much more to be done. This chapter notes the implications the previous discussions of coping suggest for consultation, education, and research, with a view toward identifying some areas of health care that need to be expanded in developing a more comprehensive understanding of coping processes.

CONSULTATION

Consultation was defined by Caplan (1970) as

> a process of interaction between two professional persons— the consultant, who is a specialist, and the consultee, who invokes the consultant's help in regard to a current work problem with which he is having some difficulty and which he has decided is within the other's area of specialized competence. The work problem involves the management or treatment of one or more clients of the consultee, or the planning or implementation of a program to cater to such clients. (p. 19)

Nurse-to-nurse consultation is a resource theoretically available to all nurses but tapped by very few (Marcus, 1976). Nurses on a neurosurgical hospital unit could surely benefit by asking for help from the nurses on the psychiatric unit regarding the appropriate intervention for a patient exhibiting a difficult coping strategy involving paranoid ideations.

In general, the consultation process follows the same general outline as crisis intervention. The consultant must first define the consultation problem; the problem may or may not be what the consultee initially states as a problem. Caplan has identified "theme interference" and a block that the consultant must be aware of in order to resolve the problem successfully. Theme interference is a distortion of perception caused by the consultee's emotional involvement with the client or some pressure of the system on the consultee that interferes with his or her objective evaluation of the clinical situation.

For example, if the expectation of the system (the administrators) is that all postoperative hysterectomy patients will be up to the bathroom with help on the first postoperative day and a particular patient refuses to get out of bed, the nurse reasons (unconsciously) that he or she is not meeting the expectations that supervisors have of the caregivers. This thinking results in the nurse's conclusion (still unconscious) that he or she must be a bad or ineffective nurse. Consciously, the nurse feels some discomfort and seeks help for the client. It becomes the consultant's job to sort out with the consultee what the real problem is. Because this sorting process can be delicate, Deloughery, Gebbie, and Neuman (1971) have stressed the importance of trust-building between the consultee and the consultant.

After identifying the problem, the consultant must deliver the consultory message. The message will be formulated within a theoretical framework and will be presented in general terms at first. If the consultant's assessment of the problem and the theme interference has been correct, the consultee's response to the message will be to produce more data. This additional input will either confirm or dispute the consultant's hunch. If the consultant has been correct in the assessment, the additional data will be incorporated within the theoretical framework, and appropriate interventive processes should emerge. If the consultant has not been correct or if the theme interference is such that the consultee cannot yet understand the consultant's frame of reference as it applies to the problem situation, more data will have to be collected until the consultant and the consultee agree on a workable framework for improving the client's situation.

The final stage of the consultation process is the consultant's summary of what has occurred and termination. The summary should be done in such a way as to facilitate the consultee's application of what was learned in this process to other situations in the future. The consultant has some responsibility to convey to the consultee that she has confidence in the consultee's ability to handle the situation even though the consultant appreciates the realities of the work situation that led to the complications.

Principles of Consultation

There are several principles of consultation that should be made clear to anyone involved in the consultation process. First, consultation is an indirect service. The consultant does not usually interact with the client; on rare occasions when the consultant does contact the client, he or she will do so only in the presence of the consultee, so that the consultee can learn from the experience by observing the processes whereby the consultant assesses the client's needs. The second principle is that the consultee is always free to refuse to follow the consultant's recommendations. The consultee may not agree with the consultant or may not be ready to apply the new knowledge in his or her work situation. The third principle is that the consultation process is always work-centered; it does not include help with the consultee's personal problems. Some of the consultee's personal data may come out in trying to identify the theme interference, but it should only be used as it relates to the problem for which the consultant was called.

Expectations for Consultants

Kolson (1976) conducted a study to describe some of the expectations of a mental health nurse-consultant held by medical-surgical nurses. The sample included registered nurses as well as licensed practical nurses working on seven medical and/or surgical units at a large teaching hospital in the midwestern United States. Based on the responses to a questionnaire containing 27 multiple choice questions, the data were interpreted as indicating that there was a need for mental health consultation on the units involved in the study and that the psychiatric nurse was the consultant of choice instead of another professional who could assume the role of mental health consultant.

The functions of the consultant were identified as being that of a resource person and an educator. The client problems for which consultation would be sought were crisis situations such as a change in a client's lifestyle or self-image due to an illness or injury.

EDUCATION

The need is great for alternative methods of treatment for the maladaptive behavior patterns of clients that develop as a consequence of the use of unhealthy coping mechanisms. Although health care providers including therapists, nurses, counselors, and allied health workers use varied methods to help clients with their problems, the methods often tend to be the traditional ones; that is, the use of one-to-one counseling, information giving, and psychoanalytic techniques. The latter techniques often require extended periods of encounter time because of a paradigm that explores antecedent behavior in depth and is somewhat paced by the variables of willingness, ability, and readiness of the client to review past, often painful, behavior. Also, the extended therapy programs are expensive for the client and society and require highly experienced personnel in the administration and follow-through (Kiesler, 1967). Whereas the psychoanalytic approaches are successful for many personality problems, the increased number of individual behavioral situations in need of modification indicates that the proportion of successful therapeutic outcomes to the reservoir of personality dysfunction is becoming more disparate.

Eysenck (1952) was one of the earlier critics to study treatment outcome data and show that clients' spontaneous remission rates of neuroses did not differ significantly from the outcomes of the long-term, more expensive depth therapies. Bergin (1966) found that in studies using the two-group design and a measure of change, that the psychotherapeutic outcomes were not significantly different from those of the untreated controls. Wolpe (1958) observed that the consequences of depth therapy and the more simple clinic and hospital approaches were similar. In addition, the methods of evaluation that were used to study psychoanalytic treatment outcomes were not systematically performed, thereby possibly giving some treatments undue credit. Wolpe concluded that the more traditional methods of therapy were often sanctioned and continued long after their usefulness had come into question because of the lag in the development of acceptable alternatives.

The implications, then, appear to be that consultants and care providers are now practicing in a time of rapid change. They are observing asocial behavior that emerges from the complexities of a social order that is highly technological, increasingly impersonal, and moving at a faster pace. This pace activates the emergence of problems that should be dealt with immediately, thereby requiring early recognition. Further, the early problem management, as in dealing with coping and initial maladaptive behavior, must be fashioned to modify the behavior impediment *now* in order to enable the individual to remain on the healthy end of the behavior continuum. This and the information presented in earlier sections suggest that health care providers need to acquire techniques that will enable them to offer an array of services to people with behavioral difficulties.

Unfortunately, because of the connotation of control (as mentioned in Chapter 2), the so-called behavior modification approaches to human problems have been criticized in the recent past (West, 1978). Some of this criticism has been valid regarding the possible neglect of human rights, loosely stated criteria, and the limited supervision of services. However, some segments of the public, for example possible clientele and practitioners of the more traditional therapies, have also resisted the application of the newer forms of behavior change because of distrust of the outcomes.

Since these newer methods have been derived from studies of how learning occurs, their effectiveness has appeared to be in their systematic application over a manageable period of time by trained personnel who are guided by an ethical and moral code that subscribes foremost to client and social welfare. The client in this paradigm has not become a mechanism through which care providers' gratifications are met. The goals of treatment have been client-therapist developed, and the treatment and final evaluation have been opened to the assessment of other experienced users. The client who has achieved the treatment goals can demonstrate achievement in performance terms. If a particular treatment failed to achieve the desired performance as outcome, another modality could be used by the therapist skilled in the application of several methods, or the client could be referred to another resource for assistance with behavioral difficulties.

In summary, the intent of this presentation has been not only to explore a diversity of methods through which healthy coping strategies and adaptive behavior could be acquired in order for individuals to deal with stressors effectively, but also to suggest that effectiveness in their use can be developed.

Personnel designing programs for the preparation of health care providers should be aware of the need for this kind of technology and methodology and plan the curricula accordingly. The statistics indicate that clients in all caregiving settings hurt—and they seek varied avenues of relief ranging from reliance on forms of psychological dependency to substantive drug abuse. The ultimate responsibility for the acquisition of the preparation needed to offer a range of services to clients rests with care providers. Therefore, we suggest that individuals explore and use the opportunities available or press for new ones in order to acquire the necessary skills and competencies to perform adequately and confidently in the delivery of services to clients and to be assistive in the personal growth process.

RESEARCH

Finally, research on coping has encountered some methodological problems. Mechanic (1974) took the view that adaptation is anticipatory as well as reactive and that human beings frequently approach their environment with plans, but the study of such processes takes a somewhat different direction. Within such a view, man attempts to take on tasks he feels he can handle, he actively seeks information and feedback, he plans and anticipates problems, he insulates himself against defeat in a variety of ways, he keeps his options open, he distributes his commitments, he sets the stage for new efforts by practice and rehearsal, he tries various solutions, and so on. One cannot study such activities very effectively within an experimental mode that subjects man to specific stimuli and only measures limited reactions to these.

However, methodological models to study successfully such active processes of coping are very much undeveloped, and the lack of richness in the experimental stress literature reflects the lack of a successful experimental technology for studying adaptive attempts over time. Approaches to natural stresses can follow a quasi-experimental design and, under some conditions, can utilize appropriate comparison groups (Mechanic, 1974, p. 39). Those who deceive themselves that in the future we will develop some simple paper-and-pencil test to measure coping or adaptive potentialities are bound to be disillusioned, for the concern we face is so complex and multifaceted that it should be apparent that when we do develop some adequate measures they are likely to be very complex ones. We must begin to specify the relative probabilities that, under given circumstances, one coping attempt will follow another. This theoretical approach will depend on rich field studies that depict the scope of alternatives, followed by more controlled laboratory studies that attempt to determine the conditions under which one or another form of behavior follows (Mechanic, 1974, pp. 41-42). What better "field" could there possibly be for the study of coping behaviors than health care delivery systems? This would necessitate cooperation between the health care providers and the experimenters, but what a giant step for both groups if this could be accomplished!

Studies that directly focus on the coping process—to investigate the varieties of coping techniques, the circumstances under which they are or can be utilized, and the range of consequences of their use—are both few in number and vital in their contribution to our knowledge of human stress. Lazarus' (1981) work on daily "hassles," for example, brings some former beliefs about major life events into question. More effort on studies of the coping process is a clear and critical need for future research (McGrath, 1970).

Several nurses have conducted studies related to coping. In 1970, Nuckolls investigated the relationships of life crises and psychosocial assets to the course and outcome of pregnancy. Data obtained from the 170 married primigravidas for whom records were completed were interpreted to indicate that women who had high life change scores both before and during pregnancy were twice as likely to have complications if they had an unfavorable score on a questionnaire designed to evaluate psychosocial assets than if this score were favorable. A study by Hogue in 1974 investigated whether or not persons with superior coping resources are protected against motor vehicle accidents and violations and decrement in functional health status in the presence of stressful life events. The data were analyzed for 416 white male and female community residents aged 46 to 71. There was no association between coping resources and motor vehicle accidents or violations in either the absence or presence of stress risk; however, in the presence of stress risk there was a significant positive association between coping resources and health change.

Bell's (1977) study was designed to examine the relationship between stressful life events and mental-illness and mental-wellness behaviors and the coping methods used by individuals who exhibited each behavior pattern. Thirty subjects defined as having symptoms of mental illness served as the experimental group; the control group consisted of 30 individuals who did not have a history of mental illness and who were matched with the experimental group on the variables of age, sex, and county residence. The tools used were the Social Readjustment Rating Scale (SRRS) developed by Holmes and Rahe in 1967 and the eighteen-item questionnaire developed for this study to measure coping methods. The results indicated that mentally ill individuals had indeed experienced more stressful life events than had the mentally healthy group. In addition, it was found that persons who had experienced numerous stresses used short-term instead of long-term ways of coping with stress. The investigator concluded that inadequate coping in adapting to life changes might increase the probability of disease occurrence.

SUMMARY

This text was developed in order to present to care providers some descriptions of client problems indicative of maladaptive coping patterns, an overview of the mechanisms by which these patterns developed, and examples of methods for change that clients and trained care providers may employ. The coverage was not extensive; however, introductions to some currently tested and practiced methods were intended to provoke the reader to investigate further the several modalities for the modification of behavior with clients in health care settings.

References

Ables, B. S. Hospitalization: Cop-Out? *Psychotherapy, Therapy, Research, and Practice,* 1973, *10*(2), 188–190.

Adams, J. E., & Lindemann, E. Coping with long-term disability. In G. V. Coelho, D. A. Hamburg, & J. E. Adams (Eds.), *Coping and adaptation.* New York: Basic Books, 1974.

Agras, W. *Behavior modification: Principles and clinical applications.* New York: Little Brown, 1972.

Aguilera, D. C., & Messick, J. M. *Crisis intervention: Theory and methodology.* Saint Louis: C. V. Mosby, 1974.

Alexander, A. An experimental test of assumptions relating to the use of electromyographic biofeedback as a general relaxation training technique. *Psychophysiology,* 1975, *12,* 656–662.

Allport, G. *Pattern and growth in personality.* New York: Holt, Rinehart & Winston, 1961.

Anokhin, P. *Problems of centre and periphery in the physiology of nervous activity.* Gorki: Gosizdat, 1935.

Antonovsky, A. *Health, stress and coping.* Washington, DC: Jossey-Bass, 1979.

Appelbaum, S. H. *Stress management for health care professionals.* Rockville, MD: Aspen Systems, 1981.

Argyris, C., & Schon, D. *Theory in practice: Increasing professional effectiveness.* San Francisco: Jossey-Bass, 1974.

Bales, R. *Interaction process analysis.* Cambridge: Addison-Wesley, 1960.

Bandura, A. Psychotherapy as a learning process. *Psychological Bulletin,* 1961, *58,* 143–159.

Bandura, A. Social learning through imitation. In M. R. Jones (Ed.), *Nebraska symposium on motivation,* Lincoln: University of Nebraska Press, 1962, 211–269.

Bandura, A. Vicarious processes: A case of no-trial learning. In L. Berkowitz (Ed.), *Advances in Experimental Social Psychology,* New York: Academic, 1965, *2,* 534–536.

Bandura, A. Modeling approaches to the modification of phobic disorders. *International Psychiatric Clinician*, 1969, *6*, 201–223.

Bandura, A. *Principles of behavior modification*. New York: Holt, Rinehart, & Winston, 1969.

Bandura, A., & Kupers, C. Transmission of patterns of self-reinforcement through modeling. *Journal of Abnormal Social Psychology*, 1974, *69*, 1–9.

Bandura, A., & Menlove, F. Factors determining vicarious extinction of avoidance behavior through symbolic modeling. *Journal of Personality and Social Psychology*, 1968, *8*, 99–108.

Bandura, A., & Simon, K. The role of proximal intentions in self-regulation of refractory behavior. *Cognitive Therapy and Research*, 1977, *1*, 177–193.

Bandura, A., & Walters, R. *Social learning and personality development*. New York: Holt, Rinehart, & Winston, 1963.

Bandura, A., Jeffery, R., & Wright, C. Efficacy of participant modeling as a function of response induction aids. *Journal of Abnormal Psychology*, 1974, *83*, 56–64.

Bard, M., & Sutherland, A. M. Psychological impact of cancer and its treatment. *Cancer*, 1955, *8*(4), 656–672.

Bartnick, R., & O'Brien, C. Health care and counseling skills. *Personnel and Guidance Journal*, 1980, *58*, 666–667.

Basmajian, J. Control and training of individual motor units. *Science*, 1963, *141*, 440–441.

Bass, B., & Duntenan, G. Behavior in groups as a function of self-interaction and task orientation. *Journal of Abnormal Psychology*, 1963, *66*, 414–428.

Bell, J. M. Stressful life events and coping methods in mental-illness and -wellness behaviors. *Nursing Research*, 1977, *26*(2), 136–141.

Benne, K., & Levit, G. The nature of groups and helping groups improve their operation. *Review of Educational Research*, Washington, DC: American Educational Research Association, 1953, p. 290.

Benson, H. *The relaxation response.* New York: William Morrow, 1975.

Benson, H., & Goodale, I. The relaxation response: Your inborn capacity to counteract the harmful effects of stress. *Journal of Florida Medical Association,* 1981, *68,* 265–267.

Betz, R., Wilbur, M., & Roberts, W. J. A structural blueprint for group facilitators: Three group modalities. *Personnel and Guidance Journal,* 1981, *60,* 31–37.

Bloom, B. Strategies for the prevention of mental disorders. In G. Rosenblum (Ed.), *Issues in community psychology and preventive mental health.* New York: Behavioral Publications, 1971.

Bohlin, G., & Graham, F. K. Cardiac deceleration and reflex blink facilitation. *Psychophysiology,* 1977, *14,* 324–430.

Bonin, C. Architectonics of the precentral motor cortex. In P. Bucy (Ed.), *The precentral motor cortex.* Urbana: University of Illinois Press, 1943.

Bonin, C. The frontal lobe of primates. *Research Publication Association Nervous and Mental Disease,* 1948.

Borkovec, T. Effects of progressive relaxation on sleep disturbance: An electroencephalographic evaluation. *Psychosomatic Medicine,* 1976, *3,* 173–180.

Bourne, P. G. (Ed.). *The psychology and physiology of stress.* New York: Academic Press, 1969.

Bradburn, N. Need achievement and father dominance in Turkey. *Journal of Abnormal Social Psychology,* 1963, *67,* 464–468.

Brammer, L. Who can be a helper? *Personnel and Guidance Journal,* 1977, *55,* 303–308.

Brim, O. Personality development as role-learning. In I. Iscoe & H. Stevenson (Eds.), *Personality development in children.* Austin: University of Texas, 1960, pp. 127–159.

Brim, O., & Wheeler, S. *Socialization after childhood.* New York: Wiley & Sons, 1966.

Bruner, J. *The process of education.* Cambridge: Harvard University Press, 1961.

Bruner, J. Some theorems on instruction illustrated with reference to mathematics. In E. Hilgard (Ed.), *Theories of learning and instruction.* Chicago: University of Chicago Press, 1964, 306–335.

Budzynski, T., Stoyva, J., & Adler, C. EMG biofeedback and tension headache: A controlled outcome study. *Seminars in Psychiatry,* 1973, 5, 397–410.

Bugelski, B. *The psychology of learning applied to teaching.* Indianapolis: Bobbs-Merrill, 1964.

Burgess, A. W., & Lazare, A. *Community mental health: Target populations.* Englewood Cliffs, NJ: Prentice-Hall, 1976.

Byrne, M., & Thompson, L. *Key concepts for the study and practice of nursing.* Saint Louis: C. V. Mosby, 1972.

Cannon, W. *The wisdom of the body.* New York: W. W. Norton, 1939.

Caplan, G. *Principles of preventive psychiatry.* New York: Basic Books, 1964.

Caplan, G. *The theory and practice of mental health consultation.* New York: Basic Books, 1970.

Caplan, G. *Support systems and community mental health: Lectures on concept development.* New York: Behavioral Publications, 1974.

Carkhuff, R. *Helping and human relations* (1). New York: Holt, Rinehart, & Winston, 1969.

Carkhuff, R., & Berenson, B. *Teaching as treatment.* Amherst, MA: Human Relations Development Press, 1976.

Cassell, J. C. Psychiatric epidemiology. In G. Caplan (Ed.), *American handbook of psychiatry.* Vol. II. (2nd. ed.). New York: Basic Books, 1974.

Christman, M., & Riehl, J. P. The systems-developmental stress model. In J. P. Riehl & C. Roy (Eds.), *Conceptual models for nursing practice.* New York: Appleton-Century-Crofts, 1974.

Clement, P. W. Getting religion. *APA Monitor,* June, 1978, p. 2.

Cole, H., & Sarnoff, D. Creativity and counseling. *Personnel and Guidance Journal,* 1980, *59,* 140–146.

Coleman, J. C. Life stress and maladaptive behavior. *American Journal of Occupational Therapy,* 1973, 27(4), 169–180.

Cooke, G. Evaluation of the efficacy of the components of reciprocal inhibition psychotherapy. *Journal of Abnormal Psychology,* 1968, *73,* 464–467.

Davis, D., McLemore, C., & London, P. The role of visual imagery in desensitization. *Behaviour Research and Therapy,* 1970, *8,* 11–13.

Davison, G. Relative contributions of differential relaxation to *in vivo* desensitization of a neurotic fear. *Annual Proceedings of the 73rd American Psychological Association,* 1965, *5,* 209–210.

Davison, G. Anxiety under total curarization. *Journal of Nervous and Mental Diseases,* 1966, *143,* 443–448.

Davison, G., & Valins, S. Self-produced and drug-produced relaxation. *Behaviour Research and Therapy,* 1968, *6,* 401–402.

Dawley, H., & Wenrich, W. *Achieving assertive behavior: A guide to assertive training.* Monterey, CA: Brooks/Cole, 1976.

Deloughery, G., Gebbie, K., & Neuman, B. *Consultation and community organization in community mental health nursing.* Baltimore: Williams & Wilkins, 1971.

Duke, R. *Gaming: The future's language.* New York: Holsted Press Division, Wiley & Sons, 1974.

Dunham, P. The nature of reinforcing stimuli. In W. Honig & J. Staddon (Eds.), *Handbook of operant behavior.* Englewood Cliffs, NJ: Prentice-Hall, 1977.

Eisler, R., Hersen, M., & Miller, P. Effects of modeling on components of assertive behavior. *Journal of Behavior Therapy and Experimental Psychiatry,* 1973, *4,* 1–6.

Erikson, E. *Childhood and society.* New York: W. W. Norton, 1963.

Ewing, C. *Crisis intervention and psychotherapy.* New York: Oxford University Press, 1978.

Eysenk, H. The effects of psychotherapy. *Journal of Counseling Psychology,* 1952, *16,* 319–325.

Eysenk, H. The effects of psychotherapy. *Journal of Psychology,* 1965, *1,* 97–118.

Felton, B., Brown, P., Lehmann, S., & Liberatos, P. The coping function of sex-role attitudes during marital disruption. *Journal of Health and Social Behavior,* 1980, *21,* 240–248.

Ferster, C., & Skinner, B. *Schedules of reinforcement.* New York: Appleton-Century-Crofts, 1957.

Foley, P. Psych out. *Atlanta Journal and Constitution,* July 9, 1978, p. 18-D.

Folkman, S., Schaefer, C., & Lazarus, R. S. Cognitive processes as mediators of stress and coping. In V. Hamilton & D. M. Warburton (Eds.), *Human stress and cognition: An information processing approach.* New York: Wiley & Sons, 1979.

Frankl, V. *Man's search for meaning.* New York: Washington Square Press, 1959.

French, J., Rodgers, W., & Cobb, S. Adjustment as person-environment fit. In G. V. Coelho, D. A. Hamburg, & J. E. Adams (Eds.), *Coping and adaptation.* New York: Basic Books, 1974.

Freud, S. *A general introduction to psychoanalysis.* Garden City, NY: Garden City Publishers, 1943.

Freud, S. *The ego and the mechanisms of defense.* New York: International Universities Press, 1946.

Freud, S. In J. Strachey (Ed. and translator), *Standard edition of the complete psychological works of Sigmund Freud.* London: Hogarth, 1958.

Freudenberger, H. J., & Richelson, G. *Burnout: The high cost of high achievement.* Garden City, NY: Doubleday, 1980.

Froelich, R., & Bishop, F. *Clinical interviewing skills: A programmed manual for data gatherers, evaluators, and patient managers.* (3rd ed.) St. Louis: Mosby, 1977.

Fuller, G. Current status of biofeedback in clinical practice. *American Psychologist,* 1978, *33,* 39–48.

Fukuda, K. *Born for the mat.* San Francisco: Keiko Fukuda, 1973.

Gagné, R. *The conditions of learning.* New York: Holt, Rinehart, & Winston, 1965, pp. 569–573.

Galbreath, J. G., & Sister Callista Roy. In Nursing Theories Conference Group (Ed.), *Nursing theories: The base for professional nursing practice.* Englewood Cliffs, NJ: Prentice-Hall, 1980.

Gardner, E. *Fundamentals of neurology.* Philadelphia: W. B. Saunders, 1968.

Gazda, G. M. *Group counseling: A developmental approach.* Boston: Allyn & Bacon, 1971.

Gazda, G. *Human relations development: A manual for educators.* Boston: Allyn & Bacon, 1973.

Getz, W. *Fundamentals of crisis counseling.* Indianapolis: Lexington Books (D. C. Heath), 1974.

Gilbert, T. A structure for a coordinated research and development laboratory. In R. Glaser (Ed.), *Training research and education.* Pittsburgh: University of Pittsburgh Press, 1962, pp. 559–578.

Glasser, W. *Reality therapy.* New York: Harper & Row, 1965.

Glasser, W. *Positive addiction.* New York: Harper & Row, 1976.

Goldman, L. Toward more meaningful research. *Personnel and Guidance Journal,* 1977, *55,* 363–368.

Goodyear, R., & Bradley, F. The helping process. *Personnel and Guidance Journal,* 1980, *58,* 512–515.

Green, K., Webster, J., Beiman, I., Rosmarin, D., & Holliday, P. Progressive and self-induced relaxation training; their relative effects on subjective and autonomic arousal to fearful stimuli. *Journal of Clinical Psychology,* 1981, *37,* 309–315.

Greenblat, C., & Owen, H. (Eds.), Gaming—Simulation and health education. *Health Education Monographs, 5,* Supplement: 1977.

Guardo, C. *The adolescent as individual: Issues and insights.* New York: Harper & Row, 1975.

Guyton, A. *Textbook of medical physiology,* (5th ed.), Philadelphia: W. B. Saunders, 1976.

Haan, N. Proposed model of ego functioning: Coping and defense mechanisms in relationship to IQ change. *Psychological Monographs,* 1963, *77,* 23.

Harper, F. Outcomes of jogging: Implications for counseling. *Personnel and Guidance Journal,* 1978, *57,* 74–78.

Haynes, S., Moseley, D., & McGowan, W. Relaxation training and biofeedback with reduction of frontalis muscle tension. *Psychophysiology,* 1975, *12,* 547–552.

Hess, W. *The functional organization of the diencephalon.* New York: Grune & Stratton, 1957.

Hilgard, E., & Bower, G. *Theories of learning* (3rd ed.). New York: Appleton-Century-Crofts, 1966.

Hogue, C. C. Coping resources, stress, and health change in middle age. (Doctoral dissertation, University of North Carolina at Chapel Hill, 1974). *Dissertation Abstracts International,* 1974, pp. 4017B–4018B.

Holland, J. Teaching machines: An application of principles from the laboratory. In A. Lumsdaine & R. Glaser (Eds.), *Teaching machines and programmed learning: A source book.* Washington, DC: National Education Association, 1960, pp. 215–228.

Holmes, T., & Rahe, R. The social need adjustment rating scale. *Journal of Psychosomatic Research,* 1967, *11,* 213.

Hunt, D. E. Teachers are psychologists, too: On the application of psychology to education. *Canadian Psychological Review,* 1976, *17,* 210–218.

Hutchings, D., Denney, D., Basgall, J., & Houston, B. Anxiety management and applied relaxation in reducing anxiety. *Behaviour Research and Therapy.* 1980, *18,* 181–190.

Irwin, F. W. *Intentional behavior and motivation: A cognitive theory.* J. B. Lippincott, 1971.

Ivey, A. *Microcounseling: Interviewing skills manual.* Springfield, IL: Charles C Thomas, 1972.

Ivey, A. The counselor as teacher. *Personnel and Guidance Journal,* 1976, *54,* 431–434.

Jacobs, A. The use of feedback in groups. In A. Jacobs & W. Spradlin (Eds.), *The group as agent of change.* New York: Behavioral Publications, 1974.

Jacobson, E. *Progressive relaxation.* Chicago: University of Chicago Press, 1938.

Janis, I. L. Vigilance and decision making in personal crisis. In G. V. Coelho, D. A. Hamburg, & J. E. Adams (Eds.), *Coping and adaptation.* New York: Basic Books, 1974.

Jones, M. Elimination of children's fears. *Journal of Experimental Psychology,* 1924, *7,* 382. (a)

Jones, M. A laboratory study of fear. The case of Peter. *Journal of Genetic Psychology,* 1924, *31,* 308. (b)

Kagen, N. *Influencing human interaction.* Washington, DC: American Personnel and Guidance Association, 1975.

Kahn, S., & Greenberg, L. Expanding sex-role definitions by self-discovery. *Personnel and Guidance Journal,* 1980, *59,* 220–225.

Kazdin, A. Covert modeling and the reduction of avoidance behavior. *Journal of Abnormal Psychology,* 1973, *81,* 87–95.

Kazdin, A. Effects of covert modeling and coding of modeled stimuli on assertive behavior. *Behaviour Research and Therapy,* 1979, *17,* 53–61.

Kelman, H. Manipulation of human behavior: An ethical dilemma for the social scientist. *Journal of Social Issues,* 1965, *21,* 31–46.

Kelman, H. The rights of the subject in social research: An analysis in terms of relative legitimacy. *American Psychologist,* 1972, *27,* 989–1016.

Kerlinger, F. The influence of research on educational practice. *Educational Researcher,* 1977, *6,* 5–12.

Kiesler, D. A grid model for theory and research in the psychotherapies. In L. Eron (Ed.), *The relationship of theory and technique in psychotherapy.* Chicago: Aldine, 1967.

Kinsman, R., O'Banton, P., Robinson, K., & Staudenmayer, H. Continuous biofeedback and discrete posttrial verbal feedback in frontalis muscle relaxation training. *Psychophysiology,* 1975, *12,* 30–35.

Knowles, M., & Knowles, H. *Introduction to group dynamics.* New York: Association Press, 1972.

Kolb, L. *Modern clinical psychiatry.* Philadelphia: W. B. Saunders, 1977.

Kolson, G. Mental health nursing consultation: A study of expectations. *Journal of Psychiatric Nursing and Mental Health Services,* 1976, *14*(8), 24, 31–32.

Kostrubala, T. *The joy of running.* Philadelphia: J. B. Lippincott, 1976.

Kozier, B., & Dugas, B. *Fundamentals of patient care.* Philadelphia: W. B. Saunders, 1968.

Kurpius, D., & Brubaker, J. *Psychoeducational consultation: Definition, function, preparation.* Bloomington: Indiana University Press, 1976.

Kurpius, D. Consultation theory and process: An integrated model. *Personnel and Guidance Journal,* 1978, *56,* 335–338.

Lacey, J. Somatic response patterning and stress. Some revisions of activation theory. In M. H. Appley & R. Trumbull (Eds.), *Psychological stress: Issues in research.* New York: Appleton-Century-Crofts, 1967.

Lacey, J., Kagen, J., Lacey, B., & Moss, H. The visceral level: Situational determinants and behavioral correlates of autonomic response patterns. In P. H. Knapp (Ed.), *Expression of the emotions in man.* New York: International Universities Press, 1963.

Lacey, J., & Lacey, B. Some autonomic-central nervous system interrelationships. In P. Black (Ed.), *Physiological correlates of emotion.* New York: Academic Press, 1970.

Lang, P. Experimental studies of desensitization psychotherapy. In J. Wolpe, A. Salter, & L. Reyna (Eds.), *The conditioning therapies.* New York: Holt, Rinehart, & Winston, 1964.

Lang, P., & Lazovik, A. The experimental desensitization of a phobia. *Journal of Abnormal Social Psychology,* 1963, *66,* 519–525.

Lang, P., Lazovik, A., & Reynolds, D. Desensitization, suggestibility, and pseudo-therapy. *Journal of Abnormal Psychology,* 1965, *70,* 395–402.

Lang, P., Melamed, B., & Hart, J. A psychophysiological analysis of fear modification using an automated desensitization procedure. *Journal of Abnormal Psychology,* 1970, *76,* 200–234.

Langsley, D., & Kaplan, M. *Treatment of families in crisis.* Grune & Stratton, 1968.

Lazarus, R. *Psychological stress and the coping process.* New York: McGraw-Hill, 1966.

Lazarus, R. *Patterns of adjustment.* New York: McGraw-Hill, 1976.

Lazarus, R. Little hassles can be hazardous to your health. *Psychology Today,* 1981, July, 58–62.

Lazarus, R., Averill, J., & Opton, E., Jr. Towards a cognitive theory of emotion. In M. B. Arnold (Ed.), *Feelings and emotions.* New York: Academic Press, 1970.

Lazarus, R., & Launier, R. Stress-related transactions between person and environment. In L. A. Pervin & M. Lewis (Eds.), *Perspectives in interactional psychology.* New York: Plenum Press, 1978.

Leitenberg, H., Agras, W., Butz, R., & Wincze, J. Relationship between heart rate and behavioral change during treatment of phobias. *Journal of Abnormal Psychology,* 1971, *78,* 59–68.

Leontiev, A. *Problems in mental development.* Moscow: Academy of Pedagogical Sciences Press, 1959.

Lewin, K. Frontiers in group dynamics. *Human Relations,* 1947, *1,* 5–41.

Lewin, K. *Field theory in social science.* New York: Harper & Brothers, 1951, pp. 53–169.

Livanov, M. Spatial analysis of bio-electrical activity of the brain. *Zhurnal Vysshei Nervnol Deyatelnosti,* 1962, *12,* 399–409.

Lomont, J. Reciprocal inhibition or extinction? *Behaviour Research and Therapy,* 1965, *3,* 209–219.

Luria, A. The frontal syndrome. In P. Venken & G. Bruyan (Eds.), *Handbook of clinical neurology.* Amsterdam: North Holland Publishing, 1969.

Luria, A. The functional organization of the brain. *Scientific American,* 1970, *222,* 66.

Luria, A. *The role of speech in the regulation of normal and abnormal behavior.* Oxford: Pergamon Press, 1961.

Luria, A. *The working brain: An introduction to neuropsychology.* New York: Basic Books, 1973.

Maier, H. *Three theories of child development.* New York: Harper & Row, 1965.

Marcus, J. Nursing consultation: A clinical specialty. *Journal of Psychiatric Nursing and Mental Health Services,* 1976, *14*(11), 29–31.

Marram, G. *The group approach in nursing practice.* St. Louis: C. V. Mosby, 1973.

Marriner, A. *The nursing process: A scientific approach to nursing care* (2nd ed.). St. Louis: C. V. Mosby, 1979.

Mason, J. A re-evaluation of the concept of non-specificity in stress theory. *Journal of Psychological Research,* 1971, *8,* 323–333.

Mason, J. Endocrine parameters and emotion. In L. Levi (Ed.), *Emotions—Their parameters and measurement.* New York: Raven Press, 1975, pp. 143–181.

Mechanic, D. Social structure and personal adaptation: Some neglected dimensions. In G. V. Coelho, D. A. Hamburg, & J. E. Adams (Eds.), *Coping and adaptation.* New York: Basic Books, 1974.

McDowell, W., Coven, A., & Eash, V. The handicapped: Special needs and strategies for counseling. *Personnel and Guidance Journal,* 1979, *58,* 228–232.

McGrath, J. E. (Ed.), *Social and psychological factors in stress.* Atlanta: Holt, Rinehart, & Winston, 1970.

McLaughlin, B. M. A retrospective assessment of unmet needs of dying persons and their significant others during the dying period. Unpublished master's thesis, Emory University, 1978.

Miller, J. F., & Hellenbrand, D. An eclectic approach to practice. *American Journal of Nursing,* 1981, *81*(7), 1339–1343.

Millon, T. *Modern psychopathology: A biosocial approach to maladaptive learning and functioning.* Philadelphia: W. B. Saunders, 1969.

Mogoun, H. *The waking brain* (2nd. ed.). Springfield, IL: Charles C Thomas, 1963.

Monat, A., & Lazarus, R. (Eds.), *Stress and coping: An anthology.* New York: Columbia University Press, 1977.

Moos, R., & Tsu, V. The crisis of physical illness: An overview. In R. H. Moos (Ed.), *Coping with physical illness.* New York: Plenum Medical Book Company, 1977.

Morgan, A., & Moreno, J. *The practice of mental health nursing: A community approach.* Philadelphia: J. B. Lippincott, 1973.

Moriarty, A., & Toussieng, P. *Adolescent coping.* New York: Grune & Stratton, 1976.

Mowrer, O. *Learning theory and the symbolic process.* New York: Wiley & Sons, 1960.

Murphy, L. Coping, vulnerability, and resilience in childhood. In G. V. Coelho, D. A. Hamburg, & J. E. Adams (Eds.), *Coping and adaptation.* New York: Basic Books, 1974.

Nuckolls, K. B. Psychological assets, life crisis, and the prognosis of pregnancy. (Doctoral dissertation, University of North Carolina at Chapel Hill, 1970). *Dissertation Abstracts International*, 1970, p. 2796-B. (Order No. 70-21, 219).

O'Brien, C., Johnson, J., & Miller, B. Counseling the aging: Some practical considerations. *Personnel and Guidance Journal*, 1979, *57*, 288–291.

Offer, D. *The psychological world of the teenager*. New York: Basic Books, 1969.

Owen, G. *Game theory*. Philadelphia: W. B. Saunders, 1968.

Pansky, B. *Dynamic anatomy and physiology*. New York: Macmillan, 1975.

Pavlov, I. *Conditioned reflexes*. London & New York: Oxford University Press, 1927.

Pearlin, L., & Schooler, C. The structure of coping. *Journal of Health and Social Behavior*, 1978, *19*, 2–21.

Pennebaker, J., & Skelton, J. Selective monitoring of physical sensations. *Journal of Personality and Social Psychology*, 1981, *41*, 213–223.

Piaget, J. *The origins of intelligence in children*. New York: International Universities Press, 1952.

Piaget, J. *Logic and psychology*. New York: Basic Books, 1957.

Piaget, J. The stages of the intellectual development of the child. *Bulletin of the Menninger School of Psychiatry*, March 6, 1961.

Piaget, J. *Science of education and the psychology of the child*. New York: Viking Press, 1970.

Pines, A., Aronson, E., & Kafry, D. *Burnout: From tedium to personal growth*. New York: The Free Press, 1980.

Premack, D. Reinforcement theory. In D. Levine (Ed.), *Nebraska Symposium on Motivation*. Lincoln: University of Nebraska Press, 1965, pp. 123–180.

Pribram, K. A further analysis of the behavior deficit that follows injury to the primate frontal cortex. *Journal of Experimental Neurology*, 1961, *3*.

Rachman, S. Studies in desensitization I: The separate effects of relaxation and desensitization. *Behaviour Research and Therapy*, 1965, *3*, 245–251.

Raven, B. *A bibliography of publications relating to the small group.* Los Angeles: University of California Student Store, 1965.

Rescorla, R., & Solomon, R. Two-process learning theory: Relationships between Pavlovian conditioning and instrumental learning. *Psychological Review*, 1967, *74*, 151–182.

Rimm, E., & Medieros, D. The role of muscle relaxation in participant modeling. *Behaviour Research and Therapy*, 1970, *8*, 127–132.

Ringold, E. The Grant men: A study in adaptation. *Today in Psychiatry*, 1978, *4*(6), 1–3.

Rogers, C. The necessary and sufficient conditions for therapeutic personality change. *Journal of Consulting Psychologists*, 1957, *21*, 95–101.

Rogers, C. *On personal power.* New York: Delacorte, 1977.

Rokeach, M., & Regan, J. The role of values in the counseling situation. *Personnel and Guidance Journal*, 1980, *58*, 576–582.

Roy, C. The Roy adaptation model. In J. P. Riehl & C. Roy (Eds.), *Conceptual models for nursing practice* (2nd ed.). New York: Appleton-Century-Crofts, 1980.

Schein, E., & Bennis, W. *Personal and organizational change through group methods.* New York: Wiley & Sons, 1965.

Scott, D., Oberst, M., & Dropkin, M. A stress-coping model. *Advances in Nursing Science*, 1980, pp. 9–23.

Scott, J. Stress and coping. *Psychiatric Nursing and Mental Health Services*, 1977, *15*, 14.

Sears, R., Maccoby, E., & Levin, H. *Patterns of child rearing.* Evanston, IL: Row, Peterson, 1957.

Seligman, M. (Ed.). *Group counseling and group psychotherapy with rehabilitation clients.* Pittsburgh: University of Pittsburgh Press, 1977.

Selman, R. A structural-developmental model of social cognition: Implications for intervention research. *Counseling Psychologist,* 1977, *6,* 3–6.

Selye, H. A syndrome produced by various nocuous agents. *Nature,* 1936, *138,* 32–33.

Selye, H. *The stress of life.* New York: McGraw-Hill, 1956.

Selye, H. *Hormones and resistance.* Heidelberg: Springer-Verlag, 1971.

Selye, H. The evolution of the stress concept. *American Scientist,* 1973, *61,* 692–699.

Selye, H. *Stress without distress.* New York: J. B. Lippincott, 1974.

Sheehan, G. A. *On running.* Mountain View, CA: World Publications, 1975.

Shoemaker, J., & Tasto, D. The effects of muscle relaxation on blood pressure of essential hypertension. *Behaviour Research and Therapy,* 1975, *13,* 29–43.

Skinner, B. *The behaviour of organisms: An experimental analysis.* New York: Appleton-Century-Crofts, 1938.

Skinner, B. *Science and human behavior.* New York: Macmillan, 1953.

Skinner, B. *About behaviorism.* New York: Vantage Books, 1974.

Snyder, J., & Wilson, M. Elements of a psychological assessment. *American Journal of Nursing,* 1977, *77,* 235–239.

Somers, A. The nation's health: Issues for the future. *Annals of The American Academy of Political and Social Science,* 1972, *399,* 160–174.

Stampfl, T., & Levis, D. Implosive therapy—A behavior therapy. *Behaviour Research and Therapy,* 1968, *6,* 31–36.

Steiner, I. Strategies for controlling stress in interpersonal situations. In J. E. McGrath (Ed.), *Social and psychological factors in stress.* Atlanta: Holt, Rinehart, & Winston, 1970.

Thorndike, E. *The fundamentals of learning.* New York: Teachers College, 1932.

Thorndike, E. A theory of the action of the after-effects of a connection upon it. *Psychological Review*, 1933, *40*, 434–439.

Thorndike, E. *Selected writings from a connectionist's psychology*. New York: Appleton, 1949.

Tolman, E. The determiners of behavior at a choice point. *Psychological Review*, 1938, *45*, 1–41.

Tuckman, T. Developmental sequence in small groups. *Psychological Bulletin*, 1965, *63*, 384–399.

Ullyot, J. *Women's running*. Mountain View, CA: World Publications, 1976.

Vaillant, G. Theoretical hierarchy of adaptive ego mechanisms: A 30-year followup of 30 men selected for psychological health. *Archives of General Psychiatry*, 1971, *24*, 104–118.

Valins, S., & Ray, A. Effects of cognitive desensitization on avoidance behavior. *Journal of Personality and Social Psychology*, 1967, *7*, 345–350.

Vander, A., Sherman, J., & Luciano, D. *Human physiology: The mechanisms of body function*. New York: McGraw-Hill, 1980.

Wagner, P. Testing the adaptation model in practice. *Nursing Outlook*, 1976, *24*(11), 682–685.

Washburn, S., Hamburg, D., & Bishop, N. Social adaptation in nonhuman primates. In G. V. Coelho, D. A. Hamburg, & J. E. Adams (Eds.), *Coping and adaptation*. New York: Basic Books, 1974.

Watson, J., & Rayner, R. Conditional emotional reactions. *Journal of Experimental Psychology*, 1920, *3*, 1–14.

Watzlawick, P., Weakland, J. H., & Fisch, R. *Change: Principles of problem formation and problem resolution*. New York: W. W. Norton, 1974.

Weakland, J., Fisch, R., Watzlawick, P., & Bodin, A. Brief therapy: Focused problem resolution. *Family Process*, 1974, *13*(2), 141–168.

Webster's new world dictionary of the American language. New York: Popular Library, 1975.

West, S., & Gunn, S. Some issues of ethics and social psychology. *American Psychologist,* 1978, *33,* 30–38.

Wheaton, B. The sociogenesis of psychological disorder: An attributional theory. *Journal of Health and Social Behavior,* 1980, *21,* 100–124.

White, R. Strategies of adaptation: An attempt at systematic description. In G. V. Coelho, D. A. Hamburg, & J. E. Adams (Eds.), *Coping and adaptation.* New York: Basic Books, 1974.

Whiting, J., & Child, I. *Child training and personality: A cross-cultural study.* New Haven: Yale University Press, 1953.

Wilk, C., & Caplan, V. Assertive training as a confidence-building technique. *Personnel and Guidance Journal,* 1977, *55,* 460–464.

Wolpe, J. *An approach to the problem of neurosis based on the conditioned response.* Unpublished M.D. Thesis, University of Witwatersrand, 1948.

Wolpe, J. Objective psychotherapy of the neuroses. *South African Medical Journal,* 1952, *26,* 825.

Wolpe, J. Reciprocal inhibition as the main basis of psychotherapeutic effects. *Archives of Neurological Psychiatry,* 1954, *72,* 205.

Wolpe, J. *Psychotherapy by reciprocal inhibition.* Stanford: Stanford University Press, 1958.

Wolpe, J. *The practice of behavior therapy.* New York: Pergamon Press, 1969.

Wolpe, J., & Lazarus, A. *Behavior therapy techniques: Guide to the treatment of neurosis.* London: Pergamon Press, 1966.

Wolpin, M., & Rainer, I. Visual imagery, expected roles and extinction as possible factors in reducing fear and avoidance behavior. *Behaviour Research and Therapy,* 1966, *4,* 25–37.

Index